The Marsh Marlowe Letters

PRION HUMOUR CLASSICS

Augustus Carp, Esq	Henry Howarth Bashford
Seven Men and Two Others	Max Beerbohm
How to Travel Incognito	Ludwig Bemelmans
The Freaks of Mayfair	E F Benson
Mapp and Lucia	E F Benson
How Steeple Sinderby Wanderers Won the FA Cup	J L Carr
*The Diary of a Provincial Lady**	E M Delafield
The Papers of A J Wentworth, BA	H F Ellis
Squire Haggard's Journal	Michael Green
The Diary of a Nobody	George and Weedon Grossmith
Three Men in a Boat	Jerome K Jerome
Mrs Caudle's Curtain Lectures	Douglas Jerrold
Sunshine Sketches of a Little Town	Stephen Leacock
No Mother to Guide Her	Anita Loos
Here's Luck	Lennie Lower
The Autobiography of a Cad	A G Macdonell
*The Serial**	Cyra McFadden
*The World of S J Perelman**	S J Perelman
*The Education of Hyman Kaplan**	Leo Rosten
*The Return of Hyman Kaplan**	Leo Rosten
The Unrest-Cure and Other Beastly Tales	Saki
The English Gentleman	Douglas Sutherland
*My Life and Hard Times**	James Thurber
Cannibalism in the Cars	Mark Twain

*For copyright reasons these titles are not available in the USA or Canada in the Prion edition.

The Marsh Marlowe Letters

The Correspondence of Gerald Marsh
and
Sir Harvey Marlowe

edited by
CRAIG BROWN

PRION

This edition published in 2001 by
Prion Books Limited,
Imperial Works,
Perren Street,
London NW5 3ED
www.prionbooks.com

A catalogue record for this book is available from the
British Library

ISBN 1-85375-461-7

Jacket design by Keenan
Printed and bound in Great Britain
by Creative Print & Design, Wales

For
Lesley

The man with no stamp is rich in spittle

Mexican Proverb

INTRODUCTION

When I wrote this book, an eerie seventeen years ago, I imagined it to be entirely nonsensical. Aged 26, I was living by myself in a tiny, tumble-down cottage in Suffolk, going for walks and bicycle rides and writing odd bits of journalism to keep me going before I engaged on some great and lasting project.

One evening, I decided I had been shilly-shallying for long enough. There was nothing for it but to begin writing a book. But which book, on what? I think I must have thought the right book would enter my head overnight, and my job would merely entail typing it out neatly in the morning.

The next day, like many authors before me, I realised with a jolt that, though I was all set to write a book, I had no idea which one. But I was all charged up to start typing, so I decided in a matter of minutes to write a book of parodies, knocking off a different author each day. It was, if you will, a method of postponing the big decision, a method I have stuck with, in modified form, ever since.

Who to begin with? I looked around my office, which was a converted, or semi-converted, coal shed. Some months before – perhaps for Christmas, 1983 – I had been given a set of *The Lyttelton Hart-Davis Letters* by my friend Hugh Massingberd. They were within easy reach, and had a distinctive and parodiable style, so I thought they would be as good a place to start as any.

I wrote one letter, then its reply, then another letter, then another reply. And so on. By the end of the first day, I had typed way beyond my quota of words, but the wind was behind me and I felt I had not quite finished dealing with these nutty characters. So the next morning I decided to break the rule I had set myself, and I continued to write, or rewrite, *The Lyttelton Hart-Davis letters*.

Some readers may need reminding as to what *The Lyttelton Hart-Davis Letters* were. They were the correspondence between the publisher Rupert Hart-Davis and his old Eton classics master, George Lyttelton. The first volume had attracted glowing reviews, 'civilised' 'agreeable' and 'urbane' being the most frequently employed adjectives, 'splendidly' 'unrepentently' and 'delightfully' the most frequently employed adverbs.

Day followed day, and my pile of bogus letters grew ever taller. Beneath the agreeably civilised urbanity, a farcical tale of intrigue, blackmail, adultery and avarice was developing. Before very long - six weeks or so, as far as I can remember - I had written enough pages to form a book, albeit a rather slim book.

Re-reading *The Marsh Marlowe Letters* for the first time in seventeen years, my over-riding thought is: *what on earth did I think I was up to?* For my first novel, if one can call it that, I had chosen to embark on a parody of a book which could not have sold more than a few thousand copies, and had not even made it into paperback. My parody could only be enjoyed by those who had enjoyed the original letters – and those who had enjoyed the original letters would certainly not enjoy my parody. Whatever else its faults, *The Marsh Marlowe Letters* was never conceived with the market in mind.

Nevertheless, it found a publisher, and came out in the autumn of 1984. I suspect that literary editors considered it a joke book for Christmas rather than anything more solid. For three or four weeks, not a single review appeared. Eventually, a review appeared in *Country Life* magazine, and one or two others came in dribs and drabs, but by and large it passed unnoticed.

One or two people liked the book, not all of them close friends. About once every three years, I bump into someone who claims to have read it. But it was never, to be honest, a huge success, so its relaunch under the title of Humour Classic has an appropriately parodic quality about it.

In 1990, it was turned into a play by Keith Waterhouse, and for a brief while it was even on in the West End with Sir Michael Hordern and Dinsdale Landen in the leading roles. But for some reason onstage it was almost embarrassingly unfunny: at the première, my wife had to drag me back in after the interval. Somehow, all the book's irony – and there is nothing in it that isn't ironic – seemed to go astray. The audience, desperate for merriment, took all the correspondents' remarks at face value, laughing approvingly rather than smirking disapprovingly, as had been my intention in the original.

Oddly enough the book found an American publisher in 1997, thirteen years after its British publication.

Heaven knows what an American audience makes of all those references to Anita Harris, Melvyn Bragg, Fred Housego, Godfrey Smith and Little and Large. From this distance in time, a good few of them even have me baffled. Or perhaps, not recognising the names and taking them to be entirely fictitious, the Americans regard the book as a purer work of imagination than it could ever be considered here.

An unexpected number of true classics of humour have their origin in parody: large parts of *Alice in Wonderland* and *Ulysses* are parodic, *The Diary of a Nobody* started life as a parody of self-important memoirs of the time, *Cold Comfort Farm* parodied Mary Webb, *Three Men in a Boat* parodied travel books, *1066 and All That* parodied history text-books, and, more recently, Auberon Waugh's *Private Eye* diaries began as a parody of a now long-forgotten diary by Alan Brien in *The Sunday Times*. The hope for the parodist must surely be that, like a rocket after take-off, the base can be ditched, leaving the parodic module whizzing on a straight course to the moon.

The survival of *The Marsh Marlowe Letters*, here and in America, suggests it has some small life independent of its Lyttelton Hart-Davis base. Re-reading it now, I find it has a weird intensity to it, nonsense piled on parody, parody on pun, pun on satire, satire on nonsense. Now that I am middle aged, it strikes me as an odd book for a young man to write: there is precious little anger in it, no introspection, absolutely no realism, gritty or otherwise, and it is unusually happy to sacrifice self to silliness (I originally published it under the pseudonym Brown Craig Brown, simply so that I could get on to the dustjacket the joke that I was influenced by Ford Madox Ford, Jerome K. Jerome and William Carlos Williams).

Parody is a strange push-me, pull-you two-headed beast. It seems to work best, and to gain a force of its own, when the author is in two minds about his target, half attracted to it, half repelled by it. I suppose this was my attitude, way back then, to Lyttelton and Hart-Davis. Half of me was attracted to their bookish, male, tweedy world of footnotes and literary anecdotes and civilised chit-chat at The Garrick; half of me thought it all grotesquely smug and snobbish and philistine. All these years later, I remain in roughly the same state of suspended animation between the two poles, though as each day passes I feel those leather patches taking form, slowly but surely, on the elbows of my ever-more-tweedy jacket.

The book is riddled with many of the small-minded irritations and grudges I held at the time, not all of which I have managed to maintain, and some of which I have allowed to dwindle. Rather like the society I sought to satirise, beneath the guise of merriment, I was releasing quite a bit of venom, and getting my own back was never far from my mind. Jonathan Raban had recently run off with my girlfriend; Frederic Raphael had threatened to sue me for libel; Clive James had complained about me to an editor; whenever I rang the TLS, someone would think I said Craig RAINE, and would sound disappointed when I corrected them. Fair enough. The majority of my targets – Tim Rice, Raine Spencer, Lord Weidenfeld had played no part in my ruin but still strike me as well-chosen. But why did I pick on Susan Hill or Edna O'Brien? And why did I make half-hearted jokes about Max Beerbohm, whom I idolised then, and still idolise now?

I have toyed with a complete revision of the book, changing out-of-date grudges for more recent ones, and bad jokes for good ones. But there is a danger that if you replace an ugly button here and pull out a thread there, then before you know it your trousers will have fallen down. So I decided to leave it as it was. But I hope for every reference that is lost in time (the comedy duo Little and Large, for instance, are not quite what they were) there will be another that has a hint of the prophetic about it. These days, for instance, it doesn't seem so unlikely that a publisher would come up with a *Samuel Beckett Cookbook*, and my list of Oxford anthologies may seem less absurd since D. J. Enright published his *Oxford Book Of Death*. In the same spirit, having exhausted all other territories, travel writers have taken to the Antarctic like ducks to water, and Martin Amis has indeed written a book back-to-front. And, in the spookiest case of life imitating art, I am now a member of a smart literary society, which meets once a month at The Garrick Club in order to chat in a delightfully congenial manner about matters bookish, and arts aplenty.

Craig Brown
2001

My dear Gerald,

My most hearty apologies for the temporary *élan* in our correspondence. I have been up to my neck (why, I wonder, is it *always* neck, never mouth, ears or crown – perhaps you can fill me in *con sum ambo?*) in the Weidenfeld letters. A new, exceedingly rich batch plopped onto my already gloriously untidy desk when I was simply seconds away from embarking on the new Dick Francis (incidentally, do you read him? Immensely stirring stuff, surely the sort of feet-on-the-ground, Beta-plus enchantment to which friend Yeats addressed himself (albeit in another context) when he penned his immortal 'What sturdy breeches have they now/Who stomp about in hope?').

My extensive inquiries in search of a solution to the problem raised in your last missive (how I delight in reading your jewels over breakfast – the sheer pleasure lasts well into luncheon!) have I very much regret to say fallen on rocky ground. (Wasn't it Alan Coren who composed that awfully witty skit intentionally mistaking 'Rocky Ground' for a modern 'punk' singer? – I'll try and locate it for you.) I quizzed some of the brightest sparks in the literary fraternity – Denzil Wrench, Amis the Younger, Clive James, Kenneth Crabbe – over luncheon in the Zanzibar, but though their various conjectures and *aperçus* made for a repast of rare delight they could none of them fetch up with anything remotely approaching a sanguine explanation of the *Kleitsmatrix* that so vexes your 'troubled tinderbox' (Spender, I think). Perhaps one should simply write to the manufacturers and ask them 'straight out' as our American cousins might put it; after all, every word has its origin, and there is no honest-to-goodness reason why *Ovaltine* should be the odd man out. Needless to say, we had a lot of fun with our rather dotty speculations. Clive suggested that it was first supped at the Oval Cricket Ground, stoking our giggles still more with wickedly funny remarks on the state of Ian Botham's socks. C. J. has the most colourful tongue. People tend, in my opinion, to overlook its tremendous *compassion*. I am making very tentative moves (please keep all this under your hat – but need I ask, dear Gerald!) to publish his very private correspondence with Mother Teresa, she of Calcutta. But when one is trying to sign up such an intensely *personal* oeuvre involving two such figures of international importance one must move with barely visible stealth. Was it not Hamlet who had a word or two to say about 'the dreaded hush, the seasoned hunter, the varnished viper who/In his very quick must forever change his target'? (I quote from memory – have you read the play from s. to f.? Sterling.)

How I envy your perfectly pastoral existence, dear Gerald! I only wish that I had the time to potter about smelling daisies and planning extensions to the cess pit. But I realise I must earn it: it is no more than you deserve after fifty years of teaching the Classics to dyed-in-the-wool nincompoops! London life still comprises a strenuous round of work and play, or 'hectivity' as D.W. so pithily terms it. Tomorrow I lecture to the Literary

Guild – patron, incidentally, Hermione Lee – on the novels of Robert Robinson, for which I am ill-prepared, and thence to the ICA for the Michael Horowitz Jubilee Celebrations.

By the by, I have beside my bed, ready to enrich those few moments before one passes into 'that land of floating bubbles' the complete works of Enid Blyton. I never met her, but consider her vastly underrated. Are you a 'Five' or a 'Seven' man?

Yours ever,
Harvey

11 January 1983   *'Bookends'*
                                                      Shuffling
                                                         Essex

My dear Harvey,

Very much a 'Five' man. Having throughout my long
– some might say overlong – life been a game-keeper and
never a poacher (excepting, if you will, eggs – so much
more agreeable poached than fried or – spare me! –
boiled) I am scarcely one to criticise so prolific and
unstodgy a scribe as Blyton, but I do think that the dear
old thing spread her net a little wide when dealing with
the full quota of seven. But having said this, I must – as
always – immediately contradict myself (how I must try
your already overworked patience!) by saying that I
consider of all her efforts *Seven Go Up Devil's Creek* the
most carefully observed, agreeable and – yes, why not,
after all? – *exciting*.

There was a lot of tosh talked in the Fifties of her
supposed middle-class bias, but as Sassoon once said of
the excessive use of the hunting whip, 'What the h. is
wrong with that', an admittedly unpopular sentiment
with which I heartily concur.

Of Hamlet I am less sure. Yes, yes, I have read it –
wasn't it the Incorrigible Max who remarked that he was
eternally grateful that it had never developed into a Small
Town? – but I can't pretend that I've ever got *on* with it.
Finally, there is something so off-puttingly *self-centred*
about the Glum Dane, so much so that one can't really
work up much enthusiasm for deciding whether he was,
as those blessed examination papers so adore pondering,

an arrant prince or a sweet knave. Agree you not?

What a delicious *vignette* you paint of luncheon at the Zanzibar. I do agree with you – how rarely, praise Allah, we disagree, save, of course, on oysters and The Nolan Sisters[1] – about the much neglected *humanity* of Clive James. His writings on Russian literature - have you read them? – quite excellent, and many of the books he managed to struggle through in the original Russian – showed a sensitivity to words matched only by his name – sake Henry – I wonder if they are by any chance related? I'm licking my lips at the prospect of the James/Teresa (does she have a surname, I wonder?) correspondence. But hush, hush, *mon brave*! (Henty, of course). I suspect that C. J. has learnt much of his redoubtable compassion at her knees, and that he in turn has taught her a thing or two about some of the more laughable aspects of our sports commentators!

Dick Francis? But of course! If this old 'much scarred and battered jelly that calls itself a brain' (how grim Beckett can be!) remembers rightly, didn't he ride one of the Queen Mother's nags in his jockeying days? *Blood Money* is my personal favourite, with the pompous and oh-so-portly Major, so reminiscent – don't you think? – of Tubby Weidenfeld.

But we must call him Tubby no more, now that he has the twin distinction of a *title* and a collection of letters edited by your good self. How long are the letters? And do they all form words? I jest, of course. Behind all that wit and *bonhomie*, G. W. has a first rate

[1] Popular family singing group best known for their record-breaking songs ' I Can't Get Enough Of Your Love'. 'If I Had You' and 'I've Had Enough, Get Off Me Love'.

brain – how else could he have lured both Arianna Stassinopoulos[2] and Margaret Drabble to his stable?

Busy as I concede you are, I can't help but cast an envious glance at the hurly-burly of your life. Here at Bookends, January – never my favourite month – has the maddening air of the vicar who arrives a mite early for the sherry morning, never to depart. Heaven only knows why Tom Eliot was so positively *spiteful* to poor April, always a splendid month in my book, but then I suppose I associate it with the school hols and doubtless the very mention of it filled poor Tom's mind with visions of the new financial year and all the paperwork that entails.

Do you enjoy eating with a knife and fork? I count it as one of the last truly *civilised* pleasures of life.

Yours ever,
Gerald

P.S. Hyacinth points out that Enid is an anagram of Dine. Enchanting!

---

[2] Real name Anna Loss ('Ari', meaning literally 'talent' and 'Stas Sino Pou' meaning 'Go Places Without' were later additions.) Best know for her biography of Sue Lawley, *Sue!* in which she skilfully perceived two separate personalities, termed 'Sue' and 'Lawley', constantly at odds with an one another.

20 January 1983   *The Unquiet Grove*
                                                          Staines
                                                  nr. Windsor
                                                           Berks

My dear Gerald,

An exhausting week, but a rich one. Eddie Tode – the basis, you may remember, for the *dégagé ingenue* Hascombe Bant in Tony P.'s labyrinthine *Music of T.* (still read today, I wonder?) – cornered me in The Garrick and over a most acceptable port proposed that I set pen to paper on the authorised biography of Melvyn Bragg. I must say I was sorely tempted, particularly as it came hot on the heels of a telephone call from 'Arts Aplenty' – M.B.'s prog. on the gogglebox – telling me that I was being considered as a suitable subject for an half-hour profile on my career as a biographer and publisher. On the one hand, I have a natural aversion to discoursing on the living, believing with Oscar that the living are more active dead(!) but *sur l'autre main* the prospect of tying up all M.B.'s multifarious strands – his search for his real self, his strong political views, his almost mystical attachment to the Lake District, his undeniable stature as a novelist, his period as compère of 'Read All About It', his discovery of the velvet jacket – represents too great a challenge to pooh-pooh. I would dearly love to know what you think.

Incidentally, how many writers there are whose surnames are at loggerheads with their personalities. Bragg is almost obsessively self-effacing, Housman, as we know, loved the outdoors and all it entailed, Robert

Graves is still not dead and Donne died with his life's work still hopelessly incomplete. I am still purring over Hyacinth's Enid/Dine observation. Delicious! I imagine she already knows that steak is an anagram of Keats? It's fairly old hat, I'm afraid.

Regarding G.W.'s letters – not a word to a soul, but I am rather more than an editor, more *un écriveur d'appareil* if the truth be told. Tubby (charming epithet!) has, as you so tactfully mooted, written very few letters in his life that concerned matters outside what one might call the purely business arena – bank managers, solicitors, printers, etcetera – and he is understandably concerned lest a volume composed entirely of these dispatches should detract from that one side of his personality for which he is best known – his passionate devotion to, and support of, the Arts. So I have willingly consented to run off a few letters to figures like Prudence Lympet, Norman Mailer, Edna O'Brien, Anthony Burgess, Kenneth Crabbe and Hermione Lee. Nothing unconventional about this, of course- they are simply letters he would have written had he had the time, but he is a busy man. Best, however, kept 'Twixt thine ears and oblivion' as Malory so exquisitely put it.

You've stumped me on the question of Mother T.'s surname. It obviously can't be plain 'Calcutta'. Or can it? I will ask around.

Your praise for dear April was a positive *tour de force*. I can't remember ever being fuller of agreement. Like many great writers – and surely we can log him as a 'great' by now? – T.S.E. had not the faintest smidgin of real knowledge about anything. But therein lay his majesty.

Where did you find that terrifying Beckett quote – *Malone Dies*? *Waiting for G.*? *Salad Days*? I was enormously taken by it. At the moment, the firm is trying to persuade him into a cookery book – Delia Smith has already penned a quite usable introduction, and of course food imagery plays an important part in his *œuvre*.

Dinner for a full twenty last night – Tony P. there, and Diana C., G.W. (he promised to write his own thank-you letter!), my own dear Camelia, Duggie Jones and his somewhat surprising new wife, the Todes, Weenie Mountjoy, my ex-wife Samantha, looking as enchanting as ever, her husband Wayne, the Snipes, Godfrey Smith (succumbing, alas, to stardom on the dreaded magic lantern!), Denzil Wrench, Andrew and Bryony Edmunds and Hattie Beeching. You, dear Gerry, must come when I have a less distinguished (forgive that disagreeable word!) party. I'm racking my brains to come up with a retired schoolmaster or two for you, or would you be up to more literary fare – say, an indexer and a picture researcher? Do let me know.

Indeed, I am never without a knife and fork when I eat, unless soup is served, in which case I use a spoon. Indispensable instruments, all, and, it must be said, *perfectly suited to the job*.

My sister-in-law died of pneumonia last week. She's already buried, funeral bills paid, property sorted out and so on. Poor Camelia is dreadfully upset, but wasn't it Milton who coined the phrase spilt milk? I can't locate it.

Yours ever,
Harvey

29 January 1983

'*Bookends*'
Shuffling
Essex

My dear Harvey,

What a treasure trove your last missive proved to be! It had me quite tingling with delight. I am sorry about the spilt milk, though. I can't trace the origin of that entrancing phrase anywhere. Odds against that old crow Milton, if I were Mr Ladbroke, which, thank the Lord, I'm not. Though one of our brightest bards, J. M. was as blind as a rodent in flight, an impediment which may well have helped him in the spilling of the milk but would have hindered his awareness that the said catastrophe had ever taken place. Indeed, *chez* Milton might well have been awash with spilt milk without the blind bard so much as batting an eyelid. I propose we pursue this vexing question elsewhere. I rather think the Metaphysicals might be our men.

Pneumonia must be one of the very few words in the English language which begins with the letter P and is followed by the letter N.

How right you are, my dear Harvey, on the *sujet* of writers' names being so out of sorts with their personalities. One only has to think of Trollope – now *there* was an upright man! – to have one's confidence in God's (is there one, I wonder?) choice of names for his scribblers hopelessly undermined.

On the one occasion I met Edith Sitwell I found her an extraordinarily fidgety woman – up and down, up and down, all the time. Then I am told Muriel Spark cannot so much as change a plug. Bates was one of the gentlest souls. Hyacinth – bless her! – has just pointed out that his anagram is Beast, an equally inapposite word for dear Hector. Hyacinth, while we are on the subject, also spent some time *ce soir* working on an anagram of Virginia Woolf. Casting Virginia aside, she came up with 'Fool, W', so perhaps God is not loopy after all! Who was it who pointed out that even though there are only twenty-six letters in the English alphabet, they can between them be formed into any number of words? Extraordinary thought!

What a life you lead! 'The merry maypole spinning, spinning round' was obviously written with you in mind, dear Harvey. Your enticing roll-call of your dinner party (twenty indeed! I find it hard enough to boil my morning egg!) made this ageing poltroon feel he was sitting there himself, knife and, of course, fork 'at the ready' as matron would say, with generous lashings of literary banter to roll around one's mouth.

I love to be kept 'finger to finger', as that old rogue Lewis Carroll put it, with the hustle and bustle of literary London, and I can't tell you how my knees weaken whenever I identify the writing on an envelope as springing from your own dear hand! Was it not Kingsley who taught us that 'he that moans of wearied existence must perforce prefer the grave'? – and well said too – but though I could never tire of the cosy succulence of our evening casserole, nor grow weary of Hyacinth's enchanting and ingenious anagrams, my heart is always gladdened by your delicious *vignettes* of life 'o'er there'. You mention inviting me to one of your *soirées* – a delightful thought, but what would you be doing with an old bore like me?

11

Exciting news about the Bragg.[1] I'm afraid I am not well up on his novels, but am told he is as good as any other of our younger novelists. Praise indeed! Which do you recommend?

Entre nous, which method do you employ for blowing your nose?

Yours ever,
Gerald

[1] ' ...arguably almost as good as any other young Cumbrian writer of his generation' Francis King in an article in *The Spectator*, July 1974.

5 February 1983   *The Unquiet Grove*

My dear Gerald,

Let's hear no more of this 'old bore' stuff: Tolstoy, remember, was two years past your venerable eighty-three when he died on that Moscow platform while attempting to leave his wife, and only his closest friends would have dreamt of terming Count Leo a bore! Incidentally, do folk still expire upon platforms, and, if so, upon which? I would imagine that with all this 'Senior Citizen Railcard' nonsense, the porters' valuable time is mostly spent carting them off by the truckload. Who was it who compared death to an hippopotamus? I can't place it.

There *are* other words which begin with P and are followed by N, but most of them – like PeN, PoNd, and PaiNt – have other letters in between. You have indeed struck a rich seam with Pneumonia.

I was greatly struck by your off-the-cuff reference to God, yea or nay? Obviously I've never met him, and therefore couldn't give you a firm answer, but I once sat next to the last but one Archbish.of C. at a most agreeable dinner to celebrate, if my memory serves, the entry of Arianna Stassinopoulos into paperback, and he came out firmly for the existence and, *quo vadis*, against the non-existence, *per se*. Herein lie the questions of a thousand Common Entrance General Knowledge papers, unless I am much mistaken. Of course, one is tremendously taken with the figure of Christ (the Bible is still the best-selling book in the world) but much of his 'message' (awful word) is surely only of use to the Galilee fish trade, and then only if taken with a pretty hefty pinch of salt. But as *literature*, there is a surplus of pleasurable stuff to be lapped up, and, despite Jesus C.'s huffing and puffing, he was obviously a man of immense charm, even if his occasional claims to be 'Son of God' sound to me rather like a bit of blurb-writer's elbow.

Hyacinth's anagrams really are extraordinarily tasty! And your own observations on the relationship between the alphabet and the formation of words showed uncanny prescience. Joseph Conrad could recite the alphabet backwards almost as quick as he could recite it forwards, but then, as you know, English was not his first language.

Hardy often complained of the cold, Pater had no children and Jane Austen couldn't drive; how thankful we should be that authors write books, for if they did not it would be an hopeless task to assess their lives.

You surprise me, Gerald, that with your truly unfathomable depth of knowledge you have never dipped into Bragg. I had imagined that wherever he pushed his pen your beady eyes would follow. What a glorious treat you have in store! His novels have all the poetry of a Frederic Raphael, with some of John Braine's pungent realism. His spelling is excellent throughout. I think I'd plump for *Afore the Chips Come Down* as an introductory read. I can think of no other Cumbrian writer who has described so vividly the struggles within the mind and soul of a young television producer as he grapples with his roots: 'Chopping at the gnarled old roots with the axe his Granda' had chopped with as a fledgling, chopping there way up on Mound Beacon as the moon poured out its eerie glow the way his Ma had poured the steaming stew into his mug all those years ago, Bevis thought of the living and of the dead, of the rich and of the poor, of the sky and of the earth, and as he chopped – chop, chop, chop – the roots slowly severed with snaps and crackles. Chop, he thought, I must chop for all my life.' Jolly good, surely? The roots, it need hardly be said, are not just the roots of a tree, but also of Bevis's life. An explosive concoction. Eddie Tode is still badgering me about B.'s biog, but as I have recently been elected President of the Worshipful Company of Authors, I feel duty bound to orchestrate a proper timetable before committing myself to yet another *magnum opus*.[1]

How much we can learn from books, if only we choose to read 'em! The book works upon the mind in strange, quirky ways: look at old Freddy Leavis, for inst.! But I veer. I have always been literally fascinated by the influence reading has on our decisions. This very morn, I was skimming through an immensely sensitive new novel of sensitivity and immensity detailing the quite extraordinary burdens placed upon an undermaid in an Edwardian household. The poor lass was refused sleep for three full weeks until she had finished peeling, with her fingers, all the potatoes the household would need for the rest of their lives. A stunning indictment of the class system that still bedevils our land. Anyway, reading it with the tears streaming down my cheeks I was suddenly struck by the memory of a conviction I had held only yesterday. With it still fresh in my mind, I went downstairs and sacked my daily woman for insubordination on the previous Tuesday. How eerily close literature can sometimes come to life…

I am nowhere near finishing the Weidenfeld letters: G.W. has dictated some for inclusion, but can think of no

---

[1] Literally 'Best Seller'.

one to whom to send them. Maddeningly, my inaugural speech for the WCA is due for next week. The Duke of Edinburgh is gracing us with his presence, and Terry Scott will be in the chair. But I am flummoxed for a subject – Gerald, 'Oh, snail with the peacock plumage', *do*, if at all poss., deliver unto me of your brightest of bright ideas. We see eye to eye on practically everything.

I blow my nose with a handkerchief. *Et toi?*

Yours ever,
Harvey

18 February 1983   *Bookends*

My dear Harvey,

I, too, swear by the humble handkerchief: heaven forfend that I ever contemplate the usage of another. How eminently civilised we both are!

Your thoughts on Jesus C. were perfect bliss. Rarely have I concurred more entirely. With all your commitments – here a dinner for twenty, there a speech in front of the goodly Duke of Edinburgh (always my most favourite Royal, or 'most favouritest' as Christopher Robin would say) – I am amazed that you can fit in the time to even *think* about religion, always the subject that had to be squeezed in between French and Maths in my far-gone private school days. All the most go-ahead young Christian beaks would set their classes essays entitled 'Would we treat Jesus better if He appeared amongst us today?' or some such absurdity, expecting, of course, the answer 'no' followed by reams of illiterate 'social conscience'. (Why is conscience always 'social' I wonder? My own is most frightfully anti-social!!) My own modest opinion is that He would be treated perfectly well. No carpenter He nowadays, of course – He'd be in double-glazing, or in the construction of those new-fangled J'accuzzis (oh, Zola, has it come to this?!). From there to a win on Mastermind, followed by His own 'slot' on the Breakfast lantern and then – the summit of His career, my dear Harvey – a contract from your good self for a Cookery Book, showing Mrs Average exactly how to turn water into wine and how to get the most out of a few loaves and fishes. With all that pampering, He would never in a million years bother with all that hoo-hah of a crucifixion and subsequent resurrection, I feel abundantly certain. I jest a little, but 'behind my mirthful visage lies the truth of kings'. Isn't the New T. just a little bit *overdone* for your taste and mine? One is bowled over by the *goodness* of the man, but can one really welcome such a song and dance over what is, after all, just a matter, as Ian Fleming might put it (incidentally I have never come to terms with Moore as 007, have you?), of life and death?

I have placed my order for my first Bragg at the Shuffling Lending Library. I can't tell you how the face of the young librarienne lit up when his magic name passed from my (ever so slightly chapped) lips. So used must she be to my dreary demands for my beloved Firbank and the Insatiable Max that she was quite put out – or, in this case, put in – by the very mention of Melvyn B. On her referring to the distinguished author as 'quite a dish' I adopted my most superior manner and pointed out to her, with just that right mixture of derision and good humour in my voice, that no, I desired to read a novel by one who was quite as good as any of our younger novelists, and not a Handbook of Tableware. She took it in good spirit and proceeded to jot down my request.

How very gratifying is your appointment to the Presidency of the Worshipful Company of Authors! Who, may I ask, is Mr. (presumably) Terry Scott?[1] Any relation of Paul Scott, the chap who wrote about India and died? Is Prince Phillip bookish? An admirable man

[1] Actor and Comedian. Best known for many television comedy series including 'Pull The Other', 'Sunny Side Up', 'Better Late Than Never' and 'You've Gotta Laugh' and for his straight performance as Lady Macbeth in Jonathan Miller's ill-fated production of *Hamlet*.

en plus variétés, but I find it hard to picture him on the moors with his 12 bore in one hand and his Picador in the other. Of course, he *writes* books, but that is not the same thing as reading them, is it? I am full of *intense* respect for his last-but-one book of *pensées*, *Mind Your Backs*, choc-a-bloc with that unfashionable commodity, sound common sense. Excuse me if I think out loud for half a mo., but could you not twin the subjects of literature and commonsense for your inaugural speech? There is quite enough commonsense in the history of literature to keep you steaming along for the full half hour, and it should go down a bomb with H. R. H., who is probably expecting to have to sit there buttoning up his rage while some screamer discourses on 'D. H. Lawrence – The Years of Repression' or some such bellyache.

Tell me, my dear Harvey, what is your favourite *middle line* in literature? One hears so much about first lines and last lines, but I feel middle lines are not getting their fair share of attention, and they are so *vitally* important, don't you think? One of my own candidates would be 'Hogwash entered the room, and, having entered, decided, upon entry, having viewed all that was, and some of what was not, to be seen, to remove himself, once more, from the room by the same route through which he had, so recently, entered' which comes in the exact centre of *A Spot of Varnish*, the middle novel in Tony P.'s delicious *Music of T.* (still read today, I wonder?).

Yours ever,
Gerald

25 February 1983   *The Unquiet Grove*

My dear Gerald,

I was tickled pink by your highly amusing reflections on Jesus C. You are quite right – my days are more and more crammed to bursting with the needs of literature – lunches with authors, teas with the publicity personages (not, as you might imagine, my favourite brand of *homo sapiens*), dinners with the big names in our Autumn list – and I *do* find it nigh impossible to 'rest awhile wi' nicknacks'.[1] And that is why, dear Gerald, your letters are so very much more than simply satisfactory. They 'heal the ailing spirit' ('Why should anything as light-footed as a spirit *require* a fresh set of heels?' I remember the Irrepressible Max asking in a devilish moment) and bring colour to my cheeks.

The Weidenfeld letters are coming along like the proverbial h. on f. I am knocking off three or four a day and we are getting a response rate of over fifty per cent, amongst them a dazzling *tour de force* from Prudence Lympet who, you may remember, featured both in Evelyn Waugh's letters and in his diaries. G. was dreadfully keen to be seen to be corresponding with the Grand Dame, and Prudence – never the easiest of people – after a bit of bargaining agreed to answer any letter I should send her and at a pretty reasonable rate. So I rushed off an epistle, kicking off with a bit of riff-raff about how delightful it was to see her, then moving on to questions about the position of Balzac in French letters, the growth of the

1 From Robert Burns' 'The Twa' Auld Reekies Thro the Deil'

micro-chip and the possible annihilation of the human race. Say what you like about her – and many have – she's done us proud: by return of post, three references to Racine, five to Balzac, one each to Voltaire and Proust, four to Clive Sinclair, three to Leibnitz, two to Bertrand Russell, one to Greenham Common, one to Ronald Reagan, one to Jane Fonda, plus full anecdotes about George Orwell (apparently he adored the smell of new-mown grass), Evelyn Waugh and Craig Raine – and all in the space of five hundred words! Well! George is beside himself.

With Camelia off on her annual hiking holiday (this year following Vera Brittain's route through Gloucester) I am left to fend for myself in the kitchen, an unnerving experience to one who, like me, is unaware of what a carrot even looks like uncooked. Has any great writer also been a great cook? I rather doubt it. The Sam Beckett Cookbook seems to be coming unstuck: it appears that he has the appetite of a sparrow and prefers takeaway food to any other. Woe is me! There is a growing market for Amateur Dramatics, and we are advised that these groups 'up and down the country' as Winston would say, enjoy nibbling while they enunciate – cheese dips, sausage rolls – that sort of thing. As Beckett is the current best-selling playwright we had hoped to nab him for the job, but as he won't play ball we've put feelers out for Tom Stoppard, whose wife is such a hit on the small screen.

I am still squeaking over the Powell! Not my favourite book of the sequence – I prefer something a little drier, say *The Upright Art* or even *The Problem with Boaters*, but as a middle sentence it's splendid. How right you are about the hopelessly underrated middle sentence –

without it a book falls apart. My own plum comes at the very centre of Norman Mailer's crystallised fruit of a book, *The Executioner's Song*. Have you encountered it? As long and powerful as a stick of rhubarb, it tells the tale of a mass murderer without recourse to humour. Do try it. Its middle sentence is 'Yes, I guess I did' which, in context, carries the same kind of punch as the celebrated fifth paragraph in chapter two of *Northanger Abbey*.

My dear Gerald, you are nothing short of brilliant! I had been toying with the idea of palming H. R. H. off with my old standby, 'Horse Imagery in the Works of Anna Sewell' but I now can't resist the temptation to get my teeth into 'Literature and Commonsense'. How can I possibly repay you? H. R. H. may well not be 'bookish', but he is no slouch when it comes to knowing what's what. '*Puis je comme, comme je puis*' as Flaubert had it.

I find it hard to believe, dear Gerald, that with your near limitless knowledge of the mountains and rivers, tributaries and tinkling streams of the landscape of Art you have remained unaware of Terry Scott. You tease me, I have no doubt. He is one of Britain's foremost comedians and a relentless worker for 'showbiz' charities – one mentions his name very much in the same breath as one mentions Eric Sykes, Leslie Crowther and Bernie Winters. There is not a Children's Home in the country that is without a video-recorder thanks to his tireless efforts. I am, at this very moment, trying to persuade him to participate in *Terry Scott's Book of Hilarious Gags* with a foreword by Sir Peter Parker.

I am at present re-reading *Five in Trouble Again*: the plot may be a little flawed (*two* gangs of smugglers unbeknownst to one another employing the same hideout cave at the same time? Never!) but the characterisation is superb.

Gibbon never even set foot up a tree.

Yours ever,
Harvey

My dear Harvey,

Elizabeth Smart is generally under-dressed and Mrs Beeton had an idyllic married life.

Thank you for filling me in on Mr Scott, quite evidently a formidable gentleman: though you don't say, it sounds to my eye as if he is not, after all, a relation of t' other Mr Scott. 'What's in a name?' as Arthur Askey used to ask. On the rich subject *les noms*, Hyacinth has been slogging away at her anagrams – no shirker she! – and has come up with a couple that strike this not unbiased judge as capital. 'Proust' becomes 'Po Rust'!!!! – surely a conclusive and pithy condemnation of the most interminable bore that repellent continent has so far flung at the face of those of us who require from a book a *good read*, nothing more, nothing less. What would the world be coming to if we all thumped out a thousand close-typed pages whenever we dunked our Digestives at tea-time? Before my soapbox sends me into orbit, I must pass on Hyacinth's other gem: E. M. Forster becomes 'Rest for me' – pertinent, I think, as Morgan's admittedly small output was undoubtedly relaxing – and why not? Did you ever meet him? Table manners at best unsound, but that should not detract from our enjoyment of the best of his writing: *Where Eagles Dare* has some of the most vivid fight sequences in the canon of Twentieth Century literature.

Like the eponymous cow, I am 'over the moon' that you have 'up-taken' my H. R. H. suggestion. He takes to commonsense like a d. to w., and just because it comes from books I don't suppose it would put him off. He visited Carstairs in my twenty-first year as a housemaster and he couldn't have been more charming. I remember well that I was deputed to show him around the English Department. All went swimmingly – he was particularly well-versed in John Buchan, whom one of the lower third had left lying about – until he chanced upon a slim volume entitled *Poetry of the 1914-18 War*. 'What's this? What's this?' he asked. I began to discourse on Siegfried S., Wilfred O., *et al*. 'What d'ye mean?' he interrupted me smartly. 'D'y'mean to tell me that these fellows were penning their rhymes when they should've been spiking Gerry? Ridiculous!' And ever since that day, the teaching of the war poets has been strictly controlled. A man for all seasons, most definitely.

In a fit of your characteristic generosity, dear Harvey, you asked how you could possibly repay my suggestion. May I make so bold as to invite myself to the WCA dinner, so to hear your mellifluous utterances entrance the distinguished company? As you know, I rarely voyage to London these days (wasn't it Martin Amis who termed it 'the acned Reindeer'?) – quite apart from anything else, Hyacinth hates missing our pre- and post-dinner rounds of Scrabble – but I would gladly play truant to be a participant in this auspicious occasion.

Life in the country continues willy-nilly. The corn pokes its head above ground and, delighted by what it sees, makes every effort to grow taller; the birds play hopscotch on the lawn, their azure hues flickering and twinkling in the steamy sunlight; the busy bees buzz beside the blossoms; and Hyacinth gleams with delirious pleasure as she plonks down the Q on the triple letter score. Our son Peregrine, who has made such a name for himself in advertising, descends tomorrow with his new friend 'Mike', an event eagerly awaited by Hyacinth.

I am told sniffing glue is all the rage. I have to go back a full seventy years to the times I last indulged ('nothing new under the sun' – the odious Hemingway) but I am planning to get back into the swing. Inevitably, the brands have changed, so how is an old buffer like Yours T. supposed to know which to reach for? Do you sniff, and if so which?

Yours ever,
Gerald

P. S. H. has just penned another immortal. 'Dryden' comes out as 'Dryd En'. Delicious!

11 March 1983   *The Unquiet Grove*

My dear Gerald,

I did indeed meet E. Morgan F. and, like you, found his table manners quite shameful, surprising in one whose prose is so meticulously correct. He loved to shock, like old Waugh. Have I ever recounted to you the story of my first meeting with the old battle-axe of *belles lettres*? We were introduced by Pryce-Jones at Boodles. Prycie then disappeared in search of Weenie Mountjoy, leaving me not a little tongue-tied. 'I adored *Brideshead Revisited*, Sir' I spluttered. Waugh, obviously wondering who the little whipper-snapper in front of him was, bellowed, 'Who's the whipper-snapper?' and marched off towards the lavatory. I remembered this incident when I heard of his death fifteen years later.

I *adored* Hyacinth's anagram. What a riotous round of fun life must be at Bookends! Admirable female though Camelia undoubtedly is (her last missive was full of a 25 mile hike in a downpour accompanied by – of all things – a New Zealander!) she has little aptitude for the immense pleasures to be afforded by the written word. But then was it not the Insufferable Max who coined the phrase 'the unfettered unlettered'? How right you are on the subject of Marcel P. Not only did he like killing rats – no bad thing in itself – but he insisted on writing in his native French, leaving some poor double-barrelled swat to stay up half the night rejuggling the whole kaboosh into plain English. And how often they describe him as sensitive!

Tell me, my dear Gerald, what do you think about

death, if anything? Is it 'the great imponderable' as Coleridge cracked it up to be, or is it a little more straightforward? I ask you because you're a little (quite a little!) closer to it than I and some Jesuit in Boodles keeps nagging me to take a look at his manuscript on the topic. He swears it'll appeal to the mass market, but I rather doubt it, even if it included, as he thinks proper, 'before' and 'after' mug shots. There are already countless books on Death swamping the market, many of them not written from experience. I'd be fascinated to know whether you, from your vantage point, considered this one (*So Long or Au Revoir? A Christian View of Death* – not a bad title) had anything new to offer. Obviously one knows people who have died, and some of the great writers have pitched their forks in that direction, but I find myself curiously unenthusiastic about the whole *pot-pourri*, don't you ?

Your word-picture of life in the country possessed real resonance. How lucky you are to be able to regard the buzz of a bee as the most important event in a day, whilst here in 'this cobwebbed jewel, this cloister of one thousand shrieks' (Shelley), one is dwarfed by the trivia of everyday life – here an invitation to lecture the Joint Matriculation Board on Sexual Imagery in Craig Raine, here a Punch lunch (did you by any chance get to see Coren's awfully witty skit intentionally mistaking Peter Jay for a Beatrix Potter character?!), there a meeting with one Michael Dainty, researcher for 'Arts Aplenty', no less.

I was talking to John Julius N.[1] (fellow member of the W. C. A.) over a delicious lunch (shallots smouldered in

---

[1] John Julius Norwich. One of the most civilised men of his time, he made culture his middle name.

smoked peach, Veau au Carbonnade Diane, crystallised camembert, washed down with a particularly palatable South African Meursault) at the Venice in Peril[1] annual shindig and he was effervescing over the perfectly hilarious new method of reading he has pioneered. You plunder your bookshelf for a well-worn classic and instead of kicking off at the first sentence, you nip straight to the back, *pelle-melle*, where the last sentence awaits. From there to the second-last sentence, the third-last sentence, and so on, until you arrive at the beginning. Quite apart from producing some richly absurd *folies de grandeur* – executed heads suddenly popping back on bodies and yapping away, couples climbing out of bed before wondering whether they should go the whole hog – this method has the salutary effect of *brightening up* the gloom-merchants. Whatever Happened to the Happy Ending? has long been a question on the lips of the twentieth-century bookbuyer, and here we have the answer: it's at the beginning! I have just polished off *Crime and Punishment* (or should it be Punishment and Crime?) and I can't tell you how one's spirits soar as poor old Raskolnikov, having been found guilty, murders the old crow and then, a free man, drops in to borrow money off her. I am no self-styled 'expert' – God preserve us from the Leavises! – but surely it is the function of literature to gladden the heart, to 'ring merrily the xylophones within one'?

Now, my dear Gerald, to the somewhat ticklish subject of the favour you ask of me in your last – and quite delightful! – letter. Dearly as I would love to squeeze you

[1] Society formed in 1966 by a small group of Englishmen whose aim was to place Venice in peril with a series of lectures, guided tours and luch parties.

into the famous dinner, alas, it seems all but nigh impossible – the *literati* seem to have grabbed every last chair. Nevertheless, the fullest possible account of how the evening swings along will wing its way to you from my desk the very next morning.

Wasn't it Barney Throatwhistle in old Greville Wodehouse's *Right On, Jeeves* who observed that glue is a rather sticky subject?! Only the other day, Miles Kington in *The Times* wrote a tremendously funny skit intentionally mistaking 'Uhu' for an African politician. Priceless! No doubt you resigned your subscription to the *Manchester Guardian* yonks ago – and good for you – but those of us who are obliged to honour it with a cursory glance have noticed an article on glue-sniffing (probably the same one!) appearing every couple of months on the dot. Apparently it's all the rage amongst the young. Needless to say, they always forget to recommend any particular brand, but I shall keep my eyes glued(!) and let you know if their glue-sniffing correspondent ever begins to earn his (her!) keep. Personally, whenever I feel like a snort-and I am, frankly, more of a cigar man myself – I go overboard for Bostik.

Perhaps it's a classic, and old muggins here is claiming credit where only scorn is due, but 'Shaw' becomes 'Wash'. A singularly inappropriate anagram for that mangey hirsutist!

Yours ever, Harvey
16 March 1983

16 March 1983   *Bookends*

My dear Harvey,

Your letters really do release 'the dove of joy from the well of loneliness'. Never, never, never, my dear Harvey, feel that it is your bounden duty to keep your old schoolmaster gurgling with delight by sending him weekly droppings from the mountain of your worldly wisdom: putting pen to paper for me must hinder much of your 'W.I.P.' (Work in Progress!), so do promise me you'll never allow it to become a burden.

Hyacinth is cock-a-hoop with your brilliant wash', and she tells me to assure you that, as far as she can ascertain, it is your invention and yours alone, but we must all work to make sure that it *does* take its place as a classic. Was there ever a more verbose wordsmith than the ubiquitous G.B.S? In our own day, only Mike Holroyd could hold a candle to his unstoppable loquacity.

My regret at your perfectly understandable reluctance to oblige me with a chair at your W.C.A. bunfight is, I am glad to say, somewhat tempered by the fact that I have been presented with a chit for that august (or late March!!) occasion by A.N. Other, namely Mr Michael Dainty, he of the revered 'Arts Aplenty'. Who was it who said that if nothing coincided everything would be incidental? Simon Jarvis Perelman, I rather think. You may remember that in my last epistle I mentioned the imminent arrival of Peregrine, my one and only son ('oh merciful Lord, count this among my blessings, that he who hast been born to me hath no kin nor kith' –

Ephesians, 5, 2) with a pal of his, one 'Mike' by name. Imagine my surprise, then, when the aforesaid 'Mike' – a bearded gentleman, wearing what I believe are termed 'jeans' (short for what? I wonder) – revealed he was the very same researcher of whom you had passed word in the massive missive the goodly postman had popped through my front door that very day. Of course, when I let it slip that we were as close as the proverbial sliced bread his eyes lit up. Quick as a flash, he dived into his briefcase, bringing out a list of questions concerning your venerable self. 'My dear fellow,' I exclaimed, 'If you wish to view your subject *in his element* you need go no further than the Worshipful Company of Authors meeting at the Garrick on the nineteenth of this month.' Feeling that it might do him good to extract some of the wind from his sails, I added, 'But alas I must inform you that it is a sell-out. One cannot get a seat for love nor money.' 'But you can for T.V.' he chipped in, producing from his wallet a veritable wad of tickets and proceeding to tell me, in loving detail, which ticket belonged to whom. 'This is for X the second cameraman and this is for Y the sound recordist and this is for Z from continuity and…' Needless to say, by this time I was a trifle miffed. Then he added, 'so I'll be seeing you again on the nineteenth, eh?' At this point, with sadly typical tactlessness, Peregrine, who had until then been quite content to assist his mother with an anagram of Shakespeare ('Reap Shakees!'), chipped in that I had been unable to furnish myself with an invitation and would therefore be spending the evening of the nineteenth chained to the Scrabble board. 'Come on my back' chimed Mr Dainty, a suggestion which, in the normal run of things would, I fear, be more Peregrine's kettle of fish than mine, but which, charting his gist, I readily agreed to. 'After all,' he added, 'we can put you down as informant, now, can't we?' and saying this he set forth with a long list of questions about you which I would, under normal circumstances, have considered a mite impertinent, but to which, as a gesture of goodwill, I readily furnished answers. So, my dear Harvey, you can depend on at least one member of your audience to laugh and applaud in all the correct places! I do look forward to it.

How are the James/Teresa letters coming along? Have you viewed them yet? Or perhaps the rules force one to purchase these things 'sight unseen'. I wouldn't know.

You were kind enough to quiz me on that old faithful, Death. Hyacinth points out that, but for the missing 'r', it neatly anagrams into 'thread', a by no means unacute observation, since doctors and poets are as one in their belief that this is all that divides the living from the dead. What will happen to me when I die? I *dread* a heaven without barley sugar, and, on a deeper level, I'm not sure I could cope with the crowds. Wasn't it that old fraud Camus who was dead set on Hell being other people, or was it his friend Wee Claude? Well, I rather like other people, and if it wasn't that I'm positive that there'll be 'free-form' 'modern' jazz playing there, I would happily put my name down for Hell. Seriously, though, your Jesuit in Boodles appears to have his head screwed on: *So Long or Au Revoir?* captures the problem in a nutshell, and I'd be only too pleased to throw my eyes over his manuscript – if he really *does* come up with an answer, I'll let you know post haste.

I'm a great fan of that dear man, John Julius. I have it on reliable authority that the Queen Mother enjoys his

Crackers as much as anyone. Trust him to come up with a method of giving reading a much needed kick up the backside! Never one to rest on his laurels, he has once again taught us that a Good Read is spelt with a capital P, for Pleasure. I have already test-driven his ploy on St Matthew's Gospel in the New T. and, as George Robey used to say, 'it works a treat'. Down springs Christ from that frightfully uncomfortable Cross, walking out of his trial scott-free to celebrate with a slap-up First Supper, and then, after all that hard slog of preaching, being tempted, working miracles and having doubts, he ends up happily in that cosy cradle *alfresco*, with all the big nobs showering him with goodness-knows-what. *So* much jollier than his misguided progress in the original versh.

Before my next nib-ramble wends its way to your breakfast table, we will have met *chez* The Garrick. I will be thoroughly well versed in Literature and Common-sense, and you, my dear Harvey, will be the toast of both Town and, I may add, Palace. I am fair tingling with excitement, and have already placed an order for a family-sized tube of Bostik in preparation for a joyous celebration.

Do you think you could wangle me a presentation to Prince Philip? I have, as I mentioned *mis-en-mis*, basked in his gracious presence before, but that was some twenty years ago, and since then a number of matters has (singular noun requires singular verb) arisen in both our lives on which we will both be wishing to catch up at the earliest opportunity.

Here's to a thundering ovation!

Yours ever,
Gerald

My dear Gerald,

With only thirty-two hours before I deliver my Inaugural Address, I have just received your last letter. I can only say how delighted I am that someone has managed to squeeze you in. Far be it from me to start teaching my grandmother how to suck eggs, my dear Gerald, but – and I say this with the very greatest respect – I think a number of people was surprised – delighted, of course, but also surprised – at the last official meeting you attended, namely The Balloon Debate at the Royal Aeronautical Society in 1981, when, halfway through the Vice-Chairman's vote of thanks to The Duke of Kent you suggested in that much-loved, wonderfully penetrating voice of yours, that we all roll up our right trouser legs and pretend to be Masons. I was assured afterwards that the Duke had taken your jest in good spirit, but I am told that those with less fully-developed senses of humour were, as C. S. Forrester once put it, 'dipped in anguish'. I am sure that all you have up your sleeve for my Inaugural speech is your spotted handkerchief, but thought I should warn you of the prickliness of some members of the W.C.A., particularly, funnily enough, the travel writers, who, one might have thought, had seen it all before.

Was it not Tony Powell (still read today, I wonder?) who observed that, 'The emotional expectancy of generations of mankind have become acclimatised to the knowledge that, come what may, taking into account the colourful spectrum of options that the future could, or could not, hold, there is, at very least, a likelihood of rain, and, should that likelihood materialise into actuality, should that moisture form itself into globules, the odds are even greater – one might almost say superabundantly greater – that what might have been described as a shower would now be better described as a downpour.'? The grace of this observation, so delicately captured in the intricacy of his prose (how coarse, by comparison, is that tired old proverb, 'It never rains but it pours') has been bashing me over the head for the last few days so 'ploughed under' (Clare) am I by the Grindstone of Work. Alas, my dear Gerald, your innocent and deliciously good-natured inquiry as to the progress of the James/Teresa correspondence has reawoken old wounds I had long hoped were buried. We did, indeed, buy the correspondence 'sight unseen' (how pithily you turn a phrase!), in full expectation that it would reveal the 'human' side of Clive James and the dig-in-the-ribs side of Mother Teresa. Imagine, then, our *chagrin* upon opening the James/Teresa parcel to find that it was not, as we had, perhaps naively, surmised a correspondence between Clive James and *Mother* Teresa, but a correspondence between Clive James and *Vincent* Teresa, best known in publishing circles for his autobiography, *My Life in the Mafia*. O how the wheel becomes it!

As if that were not enough, the day before yesterday Eddie Tode cornered me in the Glue Room at The Garrick and urgently requested that I eat with him. I explained that I had already eaten with Frank Longford and Weenie Mountjoy (artichokes in a light butterscotch sauce, sole marinated in brown ale, stilton *flambé* – quite excellent) but he was insistent. So back we trudged to the Dining Room, with Eddie rattling the loose change in his safari jacket and exchanging glances and nervous smiles with the celebrities who so bedevil the portals of that esteemed establishment. We found a table next door to Donald Sinden, who was telling an hilarious anecdote about losing his trousers on the first night of *King Lear*, so we looked around for another table and found one at the other end of the room, this time next to Denzil Wrench[1] and Jonathan Raban.[2] Both of them are, as you know, *ecriveurs du travail* and, as such, generally Abroad, gathering all the smells, colours, impressions and sensitive reactions that go into the making of a travel book. Denzil has just come back from a week in Guatemala (his publishers needed a little something on the travel lines for their Christmas catalogue) and has already completed his book, provisionally entitled *Two Years in Guatemala*. Jonathan (have you read his *Dirty Wops in Earls Court*? – delightful!) is at present writing up his account of a voyage he undertook upon the Portsmouth-Isle of Wight Sealink Ferry. As both of them are Fellows of the Worshipful Company of Authors, I leant over in their direction and told them how much I liked their last books (I have since ordered them from the Kensington Library). They in turn declared their admiration for my editing of *Roy Hattersley's Love Poems*[3] and assured me they looked forward with immense pleasure to my W.C.A. lecture, at the same time dropping the heaviest of hints that they would be only too happy to look after H.R.H. on the Big Night, Denzil

---

1 British travel writer, best known for *Robin Hood: The Life and Times of a Roundabout* (1983).
2 British travel writer and critic, author of the semi-autobiographical *Old Gory* (1982).
3 Includes the celebrated 'Poem to Myself' (1981).

adding that he had already made his acquaintance a couple of years back at a Hunt Ball in aid of the World Wildlife Fund.

So far, so good. Eddie ordered the chilled Rhum Baba (most unusual to see it as a starter) followed by the Poisson au Chocolat Diane, and I stuck my neck out and went for the smoked tongue and the Tuna Fish Salad (replete with Sour Goat's Milk dressing). As we were tucking in, Eddie asked me whether or nay I had made up my mind about the Bragg biography. Wishing to keep him in suspense a wee while more, I told him I had been re-reading the Silage trilogy, comprising *To Kill a Ferret*, in which Angus Silage discovers that he is the illegitimate son of Lord Trinket, *Light Ale with Daphne*, Angus's lyrical reminiscences of his first, fleeting love affair, and *How Ripe Was My Corn* in which Angus, now highly successful as the presenter of an arts show on television, wonders whether it was all worthwhile. Powerful stuff, I said, and fascinating from the biographer's point of view ...Yes, I added, my nib is ready to set forth on Bragg. At these tidings of glad joy, I was expecting Eddie to leap overboard with an excess of gratitude, but instead he suggested I might be more interested in compiling *Denis Norden's Book of Practical Jokes*. He must have noticed my eyes were 'scratched crimson with the claws of unknowing' as Dante put it, as he swiftly allotted me another alternative, namely, *The Jimmy Tarbuck Yearbook*. When I held out for Bragg, he became evasive and began talking about his instinct. Now whenever one of my own junior authors interrupts his ploughman's to venture the information that for the past six years he has been secretly working on a blank verse epic detailing his experiences in National Service I have always found that the word 'instinct' comes in tremendously handy, so my shackles rise when I hear it directed towards myself. But budge he would not, so I forwent the coffee and executed a firm but dignified exit, casually dropping as I did so that on some occasions Prince Philip is a little more worthy of one's time than a leading novelist. I have often found in life that it is worth carrying a small purse of irony with one where'er one wanders.

How awfully trying this moaning must be to your patience! Why Jeans? is the fascinating question raised by your ever-active mind in your *dernière lettre*, why not Joans or Janes or Jims or even Charlottes or Walters or – and why not? – Geralds? In an attempt to quieten the niggle your query has produced in the back of my mind, I immediately turned to the Blessed Partridge, without whom one could not do. If ever there were a saint in that (rather tiny, I suspect) section of heaven marked 'Penpushers', then surely Eric will be there, cross-questioning The Most High as to exactly *which* word was made flesh. Enchanting image! But alack and alas E. P. is unforthcoming *apropos* the burdensome breeches, leaping straight from Jazz to Jeer, thence to Jehovah. It seems to me to be in the realms of likelihood that they are named after a famous lady called Jean. But, as a Christian name, 'Jean' has been poorly blessed with exceptional incumbents. There was Jean Rhys, of course, of whom young David Plante wrote so feelingly when he described her in great old age going about her toiletries, but she never seemed to me v. much a trouser-wearer. Was President Nixon's wife called Jean? I rather think so, and no doubt among her wifely duties was the opening of countless rodeos, but I'm afraid I still rank her as an outsider. Jean Harlow? Surely not. I can think of no more

Jeans, so I must return an open verdict. Over to you (how one used to *adore* Bulldog Drummond!).

Entre nous, I read in this week's *Private Eye* (what an admission – but yes, I do subscribe to that disgraceful and hilarious broadsheet!) that H.R.H. has been voted Shit of the Year at White's, a title I am quite positive he doesn't in the least deserve, but which nevertheless has a pleasantly regal ring to it. Some of the spoofs that rag comes up with strike me as being a touch below the belt, but it's compulsory reading for those of us who wish to keep *au fait* with the big wide world. Its editor, Richard Ingrams, is an unexpectedly *civilised* chap, well-versed in Cobbett. His charming minor classic, *God's Enemies*, a portrait of the stormy but affectionate friendship of Paul Callan, Nigel Dempster and Peter McKay was well up to the standard of Richard West[1] at his best.

Here's another literary anagram for Hyacinth's amusement – Holroyd (how one longs for his *Shaw – The Nursery Years* – all 1200 pages of it!) becomes Hold Roy. Quite an howler, I think you'll agree.

Yours ever until the 19th,
Harvey

---

[1] British intellectual journalist, author of *I Never Repeat Myself Myself* (1965) and *Collected Journalism Volume One* (1981), reprinted under the title of *Collected Journalism Volume Two* in 1985.

Very late   *The Young Men's Christian*
                                              Association
                                     Tottenham Court Road

My dear, dear Harvey,

I am writing (ting! ting!) this missive of multiple
congrats, so late at night that, to paraphrase the late
lamented Tom S. Eliot, today becomes tomorrow and joy
turns to sorrow, but no, I err, that's a line from Diana
Ross – any relation to Alan Ross, I wonder? I take my hat
off to you, my dear Harvey, for a positively enthralling
lecture on Literature. I don't think it went over
anybody's head at all, and if it did they should have kept
their hat on, though not in front of H.R.H. who's well
known to be a stickler for dress, and why not? On the
subject of stickers, I can't tell you how attached I am to
the bountiful Bostik, no wonder that after the famous tea
party there everyone was playing silly-billies with the
crates. H.R.H. went overboard for you, my dear Harvey,
he was practically spitting with delight when I
buttonholed him in the stand-ups and with a playful
curtsey said, 'Well, Ma'am, that must have the edge over
your normal diet of *Fields* and *Readers Digests*, I'll lay you
evens you hadn't the faintest that friend Shakespeare was
a writer before tonight, shall I compare thee to a
Summer's day?' Highness or not, dear Harvey, the man's
a card, truly a King of rough diamonds who shoots from
the hip at least from where I was standing, and we spoke
of standing, his standing and my standing and most
important of all, my dear Harvey, your standing, I told
him you'd look top hole as a night and the knight is still

young I said but I don't think he caught my illusion not being bookish! 'Have you an anagram for Hyacinth, Ma'am?' I asked but by then he'd wound up his widdle and was going full speed for the exit without so much as a buy your leaf but he's a busy bee so I didn't give chase because who should walk in at the moment but old Tubby Weidenfeld who's made such a name for himself as a man of lettuce, tossing out the tomes till he's on nodding terms with whole cabinets. I may have mentioned that Hyacinth has written her own book of recipes and though no Arianna Acropolis when it comes to the Eng. Lang. she knows what's what *au cuisine* so I cornered Lord W. about running some of H's dishes through his presses. 'Not often my noble Lord barters for books in the smallest room,' I quipped, 'but there's no time like the present as Wellington once said, and Hyacinth would be as happy as a sandboy, you could have it for a song.' Zipping himself up as fast as lightning, George grunted something about the right channels. 'I'm not sure I catch your midrift,' I said but out he swung through the doors, probably to purloin Prince P. for another slap-up dinner only this time without a lecture to sit through at the end, no offence. Feeling a mite peeved, I thought I'd nip back to the assembled throng and perhaps cast a glance in your direction, my dear Harvey, to slap you most heartily on the back and assure you that not since Virginia went for her dip was there ever a greater day for English letters and to allow you to proffer your blessings to your dear Gerald for the bubbly banter he had maintained with such aplomb from fore to aft of your oration but who should enter that 'marbled dome of golden streams' but a travel writer called Denzil Wrench who had obviously been tipped off that there was a bit of local colour in the downstairs stand-ups and thought that I'd be worth a couple of hundred words as an example of culture in decline but I didn't like the cut of his gib so I left. Nothing in the slightest bit wrong with taking forty winks on a flight of stairs, surely Baden-Powell has taught us that much, but the powers that be in The Garrick got wind of it and turned hoity-toity on me. When I pointed out that I was in H.R.H.'s company, he was the husband of the present Queen, an accomplished author in his own right and a fine sportsman to boot, they smirked and told me that the whole kaboosh had broken up three hours ago so I trundled into a taxi, whence thence to hence.

Admirable speech, my dear H., admirable. You have more common sense in your head than I have in my little finger, a lot more.

Bed is an anagram of Deb. Not a bad combination, eh? What a cracker!

Yours ever,
Gerald

P.S. Do you read much pornography?

My dear Harvey,

Rarely have my ears been treated to a more felicitous speech than your 'Literature and Commonsense' yesterday evening, and I thought I would dash a missive of congrats. off at the earliest poss. opportunity. It was a veritable cornucopia of w. and w., endlessly and over-whelmingly delicious. I do apologise for slipping off early – you may have noticed my absence – but I am now an old and doddery thing and 'these creaking bones call out for slumber'. [2] Do you have a copy of the text of your delightful discourse – I would so adore to inwardly digest some of its finer points and, having genned up, come back to you on one or two items. A number of anecdotes suggested themselves to me even as you were delivering your sumptuous sermon, but my memory is now like the proverbial sliced bread, so if you could throw a crib sheet in my direction I would be eternally grateful.

How fascinating your travel-writing friends sound. I would imagine that the poor souls are flummoxed for their next locations. South America is presumably knee-deep in travel writers, and the world and his wife (or, these days, live-in-lover!) are 're-discovering' America (to discover it once, to paraphrase Lady B., may be regarded as carelessness; to rediscover it looks like a mistake!).

[1] 'It appears doubtful whether Sir Harvey Marlowe managed to reply to Gerald Marsh's previous letter before receiving this second letter. As there is no reference in the latter to the former letter, it seems likely that G. had forgotten he had written it.

[2] From Malcolm Muggeridge's twelfth volume of autobiography, *My Infernal Egotism*.

Anywhere within spitting distance of the continent has already been colonised by the Great Unwashed, and the further-flung resorts – India, Africa, China – are always cropping up on wildlife programmes on the gogglebox. Where next? Russia? Spare us that one! Australia? I jest. By my reckoning, that leaves only the Arctic and its distant cousin, the Antarctic, both infinitely depressing for a writer – rather like staring at a blank sheet of paper all day, I'd have thought. I can't contrive despair at this dearth of *locus populi*: travel books have always, willy nilly, been foreign to me; how much more at home one feels with the work of fiction or the biography of an agreeable figure from the far shores of history. You must forgive me for being so out of touch with popular taste ('to hell with popular taste!' – yes, Rimbaud) but that's the way I am.

You do seem to have been treated with undue shoddiness *re* Bragg biog. and I can imagine your disappointment. One hears a lot these days about the Martian school of poets. Who are they? Any cop? Perhaps they are ripe for an history. Methinks you should get your teeth into compiling an anthology of one sort or another. I simply lap them up. While Hyacinth struggles through her Origami Intermediate Course, I rest content on the other side of the bed with *The Oxford Book of Footnotes in Translation* or *Posies and Sunsets – Mary Wilson's Selection of Pleasant Things*. There are still countless bundles of subjects which are hopelessly under-anthologised – Breakfasts, The Legal Profession, Middle Sentences, Natural Disasters, Blank Prose, Diets, Disease,[1] Conscientious Objectors, Introductions, Ugly People, Happy Endings, Fish – and Anthologies

---

[1] Incorrect. *Rash Words – The Lighter Side of Disease Through the Ages*, compiled by Richard Gordon, was published in 1981.

themselves, to name but a very few. To dip and choose, dip and choose – an Heaven-sent occupation, surely?

A thought whistles at me from the back of my brain. Might we be barking up an incorrect tree where Jeans are concerned? In France, estimable home of Flaubert and blancmange, *les hommes* are called Jean, the scallywags. This broadens our list of suspects to include Jean-Louis Barrault, Jean Genet, Jean Cocteau and that old fraud Jean-Paul Sartre. Hard to tell one from t'other from where I'm sitting, but at a pinch I'd root for friend Genet, though as a thief he'd probably be wearing someone else's jeans, and as an homosexual he'd probably have someone in them with him.

Back at Bookends (or 'between the Bookends'! as Hyacinth revels in tagging it) the sun has the friendly wink and gleam of a fried egg lolling on a blue-white breakfast plate, the fluffy clouds bob by like so many nursery 'mobiles' (those wire and string contraptions one comes across dangling from the ceiling – you *must* have seen them), the birds, all a-twitter, tug worms from the ground as if their very life depended on it, the incessant dong-ding of church bells wafts through the air like the smell of fish and chips in a crowded city street, the roses, painted so vividly by nature herself, radiate a myriad of colours, a row of bright bottles on the chemist's shelf, and this ageing scrivener curls with his pad and jotting implements in his favourite hidey-hole beneath the hydrangeas, alone to the world, invisible to his dear wife, ever-anxious to coax him indoors to view a video recording of 'Call My Bluff' for the umpteenth time.

Your tame Jesuit has sent me his *So Long or Au Revoir?* with a most charming covering note, mentioning your name in, I may say, most laudatory tones, trusting that I will enjoy it, blah, blah, and closing by kindly offering me membership of a club within which he is quite obviously a bigwig. It is called, somewhat curiously to my rustic mentality, 'EXIT', and he offers me Annual or Life Membership (whichever is longer) for a knockdown price. Would it be up my street?

Tell me, my dear Harvey, do you rate Dickens a great writer on your finely-tuned literary seismograph? Up or down from Thos. Hardy? And where do you place Roy Hattersley?

Again, my heartiest for yesterday's address. Admirable!

Yours ever,
Gerald

3 April 1983   *The Unquiet Grove*

My dear Gerald,

I am so glad to see that you have effected such a complete and rapid recovery. I enclose a copy of my speech to the W.C.A. with which you can refresh your memory! If I were in your position (how idyllic sounds life 'neath the hydrangeas!) I would do all I could to stay put, never venturing again to the rough and tumble of London (didn't Craig Raine once cannily describe the metropolis as 'the acne rash on my daughter's cricket-ball bottom'?). To nudge you in this direction I have taken the liberty of informing the noble doormen at The Garrick to act as watchdogs, sending you back to your beloved Bookends pronto should they ever espy your brogues printing footprints on the portals of that august establishment.

Who be they?, you ask of the Martian Poets. They are a young and quite brilliant school of late teenage poets (with the odd novelist) whose aim is to see the world through the eyes of a Martian who cannot write English properly. They land the eponymous Martian in, say, a sock factory in Hull, and get him to cough up all sorts of ludicrous – and, I may add, supremely funny – metaphors for what he sees, proving to all but the most insensitive poetry imbiber that a Martian would see things very differently from us. The Martians consist of the Brixton-based punk poet, Black Morrison, Martin Amis, son of the equally distinguished Dennis, and that doyenne of style Craig Raine. I recommend them most heartily – you can whizz through their Collected Works in the time it takes to change a plug – and I will ponder your biog. suggestion most carefully.

I too relish a dip in the cooling waters of the latest anthology before the land of Nod draws me to its deep embrace. Flicking through Edna O'Brien's *When Irish Eyes...*, an anthology of Irish Childhoods, I was immensely taken with a fine description of the first awakening of the world of adult sexuality in a child's mind, written, oddly enough, by the compelling compiler herself. 'Softly, so very softly, she fingered the vestments that were before her. Cool they were to her touch, cool and luxuriant and horribly tempting. Sighing the deep, long, sighs of one soon to embark upon a journey to a strange marvellous and terrifying land from which there is no return, Celidh donned the surplice, gleaming and sparkling with silver and gold and amethyst and mother of pearl. For an unbearably beautiful moment, delicate as lace, Father Macnamara and Biddy and Mr. Cornelius and the man with the corduroy hat had vanished in a puff, and so had she. Within the folds of the shroud, she was a priest, a pontiff, even God himself...' First class, surely? I am also rolling around with my tongue hanging out over a delightful tome called *The Wit and Wisdom of Norman St John Stevas* compiled by the subject himself, with an introduction by Frank Muir. Did you know that he once irreverently called Mrs Thatcher, 'The Blessed Margaret Thatcher' (delightful!) or that he once explained his penchant for pink socks by saying, 'they blend in so beautifully with one's birthday suit'!! *Contre nous*, I have been putting out feelers to the gentlemen of the publishing profession to curry interest (why is interest always *curried*, never fricassed or casseroled or even kebabed?) in a Falklands Anthology, replete with maps of Goose Green and Smugglers Cove, memories of the dead by their bereaved next of k., photographs of Prince Andrew and Max Hastings, overviews by General Sir John Hackett and other media pundits, Falklands Recipes (Mutton Stew, Mutton Omelettes, Mutton Wine, etc, etc), a full-length guide to the construction and maintenance of an Exocet, a skit by Alan Coren intentionally mistaking Galtieri for a type of blue Italian cheese and a foreword by Sir Harry Secombe.[1]

A sticky one, your question as to whether Dickens merits one's Great Writer badge or nay. Few could deny that his characters live immortal in the Pantheon of the unforgettables, and children for generations to come will relish the rollicking antics of Mistress Golightly, will flinch at the misdeeds of Squire Treacle, will laugh and cry with little Tom Babbitt as he drags the one-legged orphan Angel Cake from the blazing furnace that was once Gunby Hall, will warm to the kindliness of Mister Sniffalott and will rejoice when Wee Lizzie, Mr Haliborange, Mayor Thrush, young Jack and all the inmates of Molesters Hall (save Hoopy, who died of pneumonia with complications) escape to a better life, trampling Mr Untoward to death. But is mere characterisation enough? Agreed, Dickens is second to none at the by no means negligible art (incidentally, this raises the question, What Is Art?) of plotting and is a master of readability (whatever happened to dear old readability?) but can one consider him in the same breath as Tolstoy (anagram: Toy Slot!), Hardy or John Fowles? Was he a Great Great or a Minor Great? He was certainly

---

[1] Welsh comedian best remembered for his serious moments.

no Great Miner, as his visit to the Southport Colliery in 1863 bore testament: suffering from instant claustrophobia he demanded to be pulled out, and from this incident he created the memorable character of Blind Quex. There is a ceiling to his human understanding, so his work is flawed; but this makes the whole intensely inhabitable by the reader. I would venture that we leave it to prosperity to decide.

You could have knocked me down with the proverbial, my dear G., when you mentioned 'Call My Bluff' in your last missive. It so happens that I bumped into Frank Muir – an intelligent man in his own right, I might add – and, having tentatively mooted that we were pretty certain to ask him to knock off an introduction to *The Collected Benny Green*, he suggested that I might care to join his team for a round or two of 'Call My Bluff' on the small screen. Obviously, one's initial reaction in these situations is to pooh-pooh the whole shooting match, but one doesn't wish to create a kerfuffle – even if it does mean having one's visage plastered with 'make-up' – so I replied in the cautious affirmative. Bob's your uncle, a hand-written note from Uncle Frank himself pops through the peephole the very next day requesting my presence under the hallowed roof of Lord Reith's establishment in a fortnight's time. On our side will be the crooner from the 1960s, Carson Mandell, and on Arthur Marshall's the actress who writes so well, Virginia Cusp, and the writer who acts so well, Terry Figg. As you know, I regard Logie Baird (why do I always want to call him Yogi Bear?) with even greater suspicion than I do old Alex G. Bell, but if you've been lured into acquiring one of the confounded sets, you'll find me on BBC 2 (that's generally the second button down) at 9 o'clock on

Monday week.

Camelia has returned from her walking tour with a most charming zoologist called Neil (surname undiscovered as yet) who is from New Zealand. He will be staying with us for a short while, so you know whom to blame should my missives be sprinkled with references to herbivores, crustaceans, and lesser-spotted newts!

I am glad my tame J. had been in touch. I haven't the foggiest as to what EXIT might be (Elderly Xylophonists In Trouble, perchance?!!!) but I will make inquiries and fill you in post haste.

If you haven't read him, Roy Hattersley is well worth the effort. His wit is well up to the standard of Lord Chalfont, and his descriptions of a Welsh childhood are memorable.

Yours ever,
Harvey

10 April 1983   *Bookends*

My dear Harvey,

There could be no more bountiful blossom of brilliance and badinage than that betwixt your last bundle of Basildon Bond (any relation, I wonder, of the eponymous James?). You have no idea how word from your good self keeps my pecker up from one day to t'other; my gratitude is groundless. Hyacinth is quite beside herself with your Tolstoy/Toy Slot anag. and is more than anxious that you should be the first (excluding yours t.!) to witness her own new literary anagram: Proust comes out as Pot Roast. H. is the first to admit that it is as yet by no means faultless, but thought you would be interested to see it in its rough 'Work in Progress' form. Within a week or two she will have stitched it into a 'seamless robe' and insists that she will send you the result by telegram, no less. She has already 'set' the video machine to record your television spectacular. As you know, she simply *dotes* on 'Call My Bluff', her other favourite, which I must say I share, being anything with The Nolan Sisters. (On this last point I know we differ, *plus ça change*, but, as Robespierre used to say in that peculiarly feminine whine of his, 'We disagree, but I would fight you to the end to prevent you from agreeing'. Wise words indeed.)

Wasn't it Bertrand Russell who first noticed that things seem to come in twos? Having asked you to tell me about The Martian Poets, I received via Her Majesty's Postal Service a package containing the latest G.C.E. O level English paper, for which I am, as dear old Monty

James used to put it, 'an accredited marksman'. Therein I beheld a question, *sine qua non*, which referred specifically to the aforementioned Martians: 'Discuss with the aid of examples as and when necessary the influence of Black Morrison in forming The Martians into a coherent unit of socially, linguistically and morally aware human beings striving to come to terms with their surroundings using the simplest possible words' OR ' "My sister's vagina is like a coalscuttle" discuss Craig Raine's use of the word "sister" ' OR " ' Don't gob your phlegm in the condom" – to what extent is Martin Amis an overtly moral writer?' A far cry, I think you will agree, from Chaucer's use of irony in the Merchant's Tale, so I am going to have to swat up to no small extent before allotting my ticks and crosses to their appropriate places *à la plage*.

What a delicious sliver of O'Brien. My own childhood lasted, as far as I recollect, the requisite number of years, but I can't remember *my* sexuality *ever* being awoken. I remember the smell of muffins on the griddle; the gentle yank of the old yew door as Mr Gubbins came to partake of elevenses; the swish and hum of the sunsets (how much more *sunsettish* they were then); the crank and yelp of my goldfish swimming round, round, round, his crystal cage; the almost quizzical aroma of cabbage a-boil; the sight of my sister resplendent in her myriad hues of green and orange at her First Communion; the fear I felt on entering Dr Arbuthnot's consulting room – how vast it seemed then! – for my first test for colour blindness; the cavernous warmth of my mother's chest as she comforted me after my taunting from the village lads; the pride I took in maintaining a Commonplace Book of my toenail clippings, and the little fantasies I would invent for each and every one of them – these are the treasures I keep in 'the rickety storehouse of the mind', these are the mementoes which succour my waking hours. I'll lay you good odds that if one were to collar Mr Average as he stumbles down the High Street on a Saturday morning and cross-question him on his kiddy-memories, the awakening to the world of sex would be *in absentia* from his roll call of *trompe l'oeil*. 'Nah, Guv,' he would riposte, 'Oi'm'a'tellin'yer, it nevver entered moy 'ed.' This is not to deny the right of all those gifted ('Spare us the gifted!' – Ronnie Knox) young novelists to trot out their *historia sexualis* – for where would the world of letters be without them? – but it is to volunteer the opinion that those of us who prefer instead to curl up with our Kingsley or our Carroll should be entitled so to do. Do you stand behind me on this one, my dear Harvey?

I *long* to leaf through your Falklands tome. What a deliciously *decent* war that was, never outstaying its welcome, attending to the dull old underdog, telling the swarthy gatecrasher 'remove your hands from my daughter!' and helping with the washing up afterwards. I *dote* on Mrs T., and only wish I could inveigle her in to out-sort *my* household accounts which lie higgledy-piggledy around my study, hugger-mugger with an invading army of Hyacinth's *detritus*, namely five wrappers from Mr Walls' 'Choc Bars' stapled together to form an incomplete model of The Eiffel Tower *re* last week's 'Blue Peter', one signed photograph of one 'Fred Housego' who to me looks for all the world like a London cabbie, three foolscap sheets of snippets of H.'s beloved General Knowledge written in longhand, a bill for £95 from a local taxi firm for services rendered during H.'s fruitless search for a Golden Hair, sundry back numbers of *Competitor's Journal* and *Psychic News* and twenty-five packets of Golden Wonder potato crisps replete with a 'special offer' for the pocket edition of the O.E.D. Was ever Will Shakespeare's desk so laden?

Following your high praise for Roy Hattersley, I have withdrawn the omnibus edition of his collected pieces, *The Many Faces of Roy Hattersley* from the Shuffling library. It appears to be very well translated indeed.

A New Zealander in the house! Well I never, to paraphrase the immortal Gracie Fields. I am told they get very excited by all our modern appliances, so do show him your radio or television, though one could probably fob him with something as matter-of-fact (to us, don't forget) as an electric toaster.

My warmest regards to Camelia,

Yours ever,
Gerald

My dear Gerald,

The Weidenfeld letters are coming on apace. G.W. was a little peeved at the lack of political hobnobbing in the first batch, so I sent off fifty or so letters to M.P.s of all persuasions raising topical and long-term issues in a tone that radiated *savoir-faire* and *bonhomie*, signing them as per u., from the Great Man Himself. We have had a whopping success! Every single M.P. has taken up the challenge, and though most of them have replied in a relatively unexceptional manner ('Thank you for your letter. I have taken careful note of the views expressed therein. Should you have any problem requiring my help please do not hesitate to contact me. With best wishes …') one or two, perhaps motivated by a suspicion that their words of w. will be soon wedged between hard-covers, have responded with fuller statements on a variety of subjects.

It emerges that Gerald Kaufman's favourite flower is the anemone, that Selwyn Gummer has a soft spot for June Whitfield, that Tam Dalyell did *not* enjoy the Falklands war as much as we both did, that Enoch Powell's favourite Tintin book is *The Crab With The Golden Claw*, that Teddy Taylor is fond of children, that Renee Short will never appear naked, even if it is artistically valid, that Norman Fowler enjoys a laugh as much as the next man and that Cyril Smith has a lot of time for the post-Impressionists. I need hardly tell you that George is now strutting around like the proverbial cat's mother, and he thinks we'll be able to add an extra pound to the cover price.

Hurrah for the start of the cricket season! Was ever there a sound so delightful as the bounce of ball on wood? As long as I live, I will never forget the innings of the legendary Harry 'Harry' Harris in the 1956 Australia Test at Edgbaston. England were 36 for 4 and we needed 93 runs in little over half an hour to wrest the Ashes from the Aussies. In comes Harry, all five foot eleven inches of him, to a change of over. Squawky Henderson, facing, makes a quick one with a slice to long, leaving Harry with 92 to make in just under the half hour. It was a cloudy day, but occasionally the sun would send down a ray to bob and trip over the grassy stretches of the freshly mown pitch, as green as a whistle, as smooth as butter. Percy Osterman, long legs himself, to bowl, when quick as the proverbial the umpire stops play. With half an hour or less to go, that's a serious matter, and there erupted the first murmurings of consternation amongst the players. 'Your bat,' boomed out the voice of the umpire, 'Mr Harris, you've forgotten your bat'. A stunned hush descended. He was dead right. Harry 'Harry' Harris *had* forgotten his bat. No one knew where to look. Silly mid-off let out a nervous giggle. At last, after a wait which seemed like seconds, Harry replied. 'No, sir, I have not forgotten my bat,' he said, 'I have it on me'. So saying, he stripped off his whites and standing on one leg, bare save for his bloomers, began to unscrew t'other leg. Well! A tangible silence hung over the pitch like a raincoat from a hanger. Without so much as an expression on his crusty face, Harry held the leg – which later proved to be wooden – in both hands and, taking up his familiar middle-and-off stance shouted out tauntingly at the bowler, 'C'mon, then, Perce, chuck me your worst!' Osterman looks inquiringly at the umpire, who, after a moment's hesitation, declares, 'There is indeed nothing in the Official Rules of Cricket as laid down by the Marylebone Cricket Club to prevent the use of a leg or any part thereof as a bat suitable for play both in the United Kingdom and beyond. Let play continue!' So, with nigh on twenty minutes left to play, Harry went on to score nine fours (two off the ankle), twenty-one singles and six sixes, thus winning England back the Ashes in what must surely have been the most unorthodox innings in cricketing history. He deservedly won the Man of the Match award and was later presented with a plaque from the Allied Hoppers Federation of Great Britain. It emerged that he had lost his leg two weeks previously during an argument over the Bodyline tour with Clive James.

How immensely trying for you must be the prospect of all those batches of essays on the admirable Martians by hundreds of fourth form Kevins and Tracys. Perhaps it would place 'balm on your oft-tormented brain'[1] if I were, so to speak, to place the boot on the other foot and set you a teaser to kick about the well-stocked library of your mind. The name of Kenneth Crabbe is no stranger to our correspondence. He is, as you know, one of our 20 Best Young Novelists, and hats off to him for that. Thus far, he has written one novel, *Angela's Gone Funny,* which was described by Hermione Lee as 'a dazzling indictment of the nuclear holocaust', a volume of short stories entitled *Scraping the Barrel*, and, with Bel Mooney, he had edited a collection of sapphist prose,

[1] *Hamlet* 1221, act 2 Scene 3.

Near Miss. He is understandably keen that his new novel, a macabre love story of chilling unease, merits individual reviews in the Sunday 'heavies' rather than be lumped together with the Steve Oiks and Beth Borings of this world, and for this reason he wants to mirror its classic status with a title derived from Shakespeare. We have both been perusing the Bard with our eyes skinned, but blow me down if every last available phrase from the Complete W's hasn't already been purloined by one literary vulture or another to lend distinction to *their* slim vols. At one juncture we thought we had chanced upon a fresh Shakespearean phrase which, while not first or even second class, at least had the quality of having had No Previous Owners when we are caught short by none other than Tony Powell (still read today? I wonder) who bags the blessed quote – *O, How the Wheel Becomes It!* – for his new yarn. Fearfully irritating, eh? And this, my dear Gerald, is where you enter. Having dawdled in the back-alleys of Shakespeare's less worthy collaborations and bosh shots, you are the ideal chap to come up with a quote that has evaded the eyes of generations of hungry nib-scratchers. *Do* have a crack at it should the fancy take you, as I have no doubt it will.

The infinitesimal buzzings and whirrings of your Hyacinth's truly idiosyncratic mind will never cease to amaze, amuse and – yes – impress me. I too enjoy dipping my toes in the ocean of General Knowledge once in a while. Only yesterday I was reading a book devoted to the fascinating subj. of the Canadian Redwood. I was reading it not from any sense of professional or personal pleasure, you understand, but purely and simply *because I wanted to.* Wasn't it the great and good Dr Johnson who first surmised that if no one could read, there would be very little point in anyone bothering to write? Sage words indeed. Did you know it would only take 3,450,000 Canadian Redwoods balanced atop one t'other to reach the moon? Ah! The Joy of Knowledge! Do pass the info. on to dear H.

With your eagle eyes you might have noticed a change of nomenclature at the summit of this epistle. From this you would be right to surmise that I have, for this week, changed not only my writing-paper (never note-paper, if you please!) but also my address. Our antipodean friend 'Neil' is what is known as a 'Do It Yourself' aficionado, so C. and he are redecorating the house from t. to b., their only condition being that Yours t. clears off. The Garrick was fully booked for the Videos Nasty Federation conference, so I am lumbered with a bolthole in the backwaters.

How extraordinary to think that the next time you'll set eyes on me will be courtesy of the cathode ray! Where *will* it all end?

Yours ever,
Harvey

28 April 1983   *Bookends*

My dear Harvey,

Superb! Superb!! Superb!!! Hyacinth and I were positively bubbling with excitement all day in hushed expectancy at your *debut* on C. My B. Over a cup of lemon tea and a digestive at elevenses I had to dissuade H. from the action that were she to 'switch on' the gogglebox earlier we would be able to view C. My B. all the sooner. Though always hot on Truth, and almost overheated on Language, she has never been a fool for logic *pace* Alfie Ayer.[1] I flatter you not when I tell you we nevertheless switched on the infernal machine a full two hours before, eyes a-goggle, chins a-quiver, knees a-kimbo, happily viewing an Open University programme on race relations in Streatham and an Anita Harris[2] special before fully settling down for *le grand marnier*. My dear Harvey, you were quite charming, and Hyacinth is still dropping your delicious word 'Thistlebug' (who would *ever* have guessed that it was an insect to be found on the Scottish moors?) in her conversation at every available juncture. The dear old thing has been singing your p.'s ever since I chucked one or two of your most generous compliments in her direction (was it not Carlyle who said that 'the human race feels greater preference for a kindly word than ever it does for a chiding' or was it Swindon?) and she is in Seventh – or

[1] A. J. Ayer, singer and entertainer. 'Language, Truth and Logic' reached number 8 in October, 1967.
[2] Anita Harris, philosopher and author of the seminal *Just Loving You*.

even Eighth (!!) Heaven at the revelation that you too take to General Knowledge like a duck to H_2O. Loath as I am to become a mere conduit for the nefarious natter of you two high-brows, I did undertake to promise H. that I would bung you a line *re* her tossing and turning in the warm pastures of G.K. Following your quite brilliant unearthing of the Canadian Redwood (no relation, surely, of Caroline Blackwood?!) and its proximity to the moon, Hyacinth has been buried in the leather-bounds genning up on the gainsaid Thistlebug and its proximity to the ground. Standing at its fullest height, its body is a paltry .000038th of an inch from *terra firma*, the equivalent of only two pages of George Eliot's *Middlemarch*, presuming the chosen edition had no scholarly introduction of any sort.

Your splendid vignette of the uxorious uniped Mr Harris (admirable fellow!) fills an hiatus in my stock of cricket anecdotage. Was it not the late, great, Tony Greig who perceived that, without bat and ball, cricket would be a much diminished game? And how very right he was. A similar story to your own immortal concerns Ralph 'Beans' Leadbitter, number two batsman for England in the early 'Thirties. 'Beans' (so named because of a barely controllable penchant for the said veg.!) was also a dab hand with a ball, and, at the start of the third day of the 1931 Test against New Zealand, he was due to bowl. The fielders were in position, close in around the demon Spinoza from Auckland, and there was a tingle of expectancy zipping through the packed crowd. The hazy sun drenched all around with its weary glow, transforming the crowd, from a distance, into so much scrambled egg. The umpire, a man by the name of Deben, called for silence and signalled play to begin.

Spinoza takes up his stance. The fielders crouch, ready for the big one. Beans begins his famously long run-up. One pace...two...three...four...five... – then suddenly, 'Halt!' shouts Deben, his arm a-stretch. A question mark hangs over the pitch. 'Mr Leadbitter,' says Deben in his piercing twang of a voice, his right eye settling in to its nervous twitch, 'Mr Leadbitter, you have forgotten your ball.' A stunned hush descended. He was right. Ralph 'Beans' Leadbitter *had* forgotten his ball. But – 'Sir,' says Leadbitter, 'Your assumption is incorrect. I carry the ball with me.' And, so saying, he placed both his hands just below his ears and began to unscrew his head, going on to knock N.Z. all out for fifty three. It later emerged that he had lost his head in a row with 'Donger' James, Clive James's alleged father. 'The headless man must need wear no hat' as the Indian sage Kahlil Karmen states in his short but considerable pamphlet, *Thyme with the Sage*.

I fully sympathise with the *bisque* into which your Mr Crabbe has plunged himself. The Naming of the Novel has always been a jammy business, and must be all the jammier now that the Bard has run dry. I have approached the prob. with high seriousness, my antennae ready to pounce on any unescorted quotation (the whole kaboosh lending, as you suggested it might, welcome respite from the G.C.E. gibberish which 'now plagues my waking hours') and I think I have hit upon two which might be of u. 'To Lacedaemon did my land extend' (*Timon of Athens*, Act Two, Scene Two) has a certain chill to it, and, as far as I know, is thus far unplundered. Alternatively, 'Tis true: where is He, Denny?' (*Henry the Eighth*, Act Five, Scene One) might suit, especially if there is a Dennis or Denise in the book. If neither of these proves to be of use, I suggest we spread our net to include Marlowe and Tourneur (by way of Datchet and Slough? I jest). I quite agree with you both that W.S. adds a certain *savoir faire* to the proceedings, adding weight to my long-held opinion that had he not made such a go of being a playwright he could have found healthy employment as a book packager.

Your Johnson *bon mot* was blissfully priceless, and, as always with the wide-girthed seer, bursting with *sound commonsense*. Would one of our so-called Moderns like Ian McEwan rate the stationing of a Boswell on his left shoulder ready to transcribe his every cough and wheeze? I think not. But there was Dr J., *café au lait* at hand, spouting maxims, truisms, endomorphs, platitudes and spittle in some inn outside the then Brand's Hatch, and there was the goodly Boswell quilling it down, and here we are, four hundred years later, lapping it up. Bountiful image! Of the many remarks the malodorous Doctor made about literature, the one I carry in the weskit pocket of my mind is this: 'A book of a hundred pages is only half as long as a book of two hundred pages, yet he is a wise man who reads them both.'

Celui-ci, ma cuisine. I have been dipping into your J's book on death, and find it fascinating – more of a 'how to' than a 'what then' book, but muscular, gripping and snappy. My initial advice would be to publish and be damned, but stay your hand 'til I've supped a wee dram more. Any news on the EXIT front?

Once again, three cheers on the perf.

Yours ever,
Gerald

P.S. Hyacinth begs me to inform you that Freud anagrams into Fred U. (!) and that she is pretty sure that Tolstoy becomes Toadstool – no fit end for that renowned wordsmith, I feel(!!).

7 May 1983   *The Garrick Club*

My dear Gerald,

I delight in your delight at my first stab as a telly 'personality', and I am positively crowing at Hyacinth's adoption of my delectable 'Thistlebug' and the most interesting paraphernalia she has uprooted on it.

What very large feet some writers have! Henry James – 10½, Arnold Bennett – 11, Charlotte Brontë – 9, Nathaniel Hawthorne – 11, W. H. Auden 10½, Conan Doyle – 12, and Kipling – 10½. Why do you think this might be? If I might posit a solution, I'd stick my neck out and put it down to all the real life they must first observe before putting pen to paper if their proposed masterpieces are to succeed. For this, they must run around knocking on ordinary people's doors, espying farmers mucking out duckponds, garnering information on the nub of life from tramps, schoolmasters, tycoons, publicans, nuns, bicycle manufacturers, shop assistants – the lot. Only the most sure-footed could cope with so punishing a routine, and those with the bare minimum in the foot line would fall by the wayside before completing the briefest stanza of Haiku. *Ergo*, the fuller foot will out. I bring this theory – and it *is* still only a theory – to your ever-inquisitive little brain, my dear G., as I am booked in to deliver a paper to the British Paedophile Society on any literary topic related to their own special interests. They floated the idea of J. M. Barrie, though for no reason upon which I can place my finger, considering he took a 7½ shoe and had little or no problem with chilblains, verrucas, cramp, etcetera, etcetera. If you broadly concur with my gist, could you dredge your memory for any entertaining musings you may have on the subj. of 'Sock it to Me – Writers and their Feet'. The meeting – at the Garrick and then afterwards at a club called 'Playland' just off Leicester Square – isn't due for another month, so you can afford to mull awhile.

You will notice, my dear Gerald, that my writing-paper this week carries at its head the nomenclature of The Garrick Club. You may further perceive that contrary to expectation I am not resident at my dear desk. I have had word from Camelia that she and 'Neil' are unlikely to finish the redecoration for at least six months, within which time I am *persona non grata au maison*, so I have retreated here with a few of my precious books – including, incidentally, the new Clive James novel (superb! a stunning indictment of television critics, journalists and media 'personalities'), the eighth vol. of Frank Longford's splendid autobiography entitled *A Grain of Wheat and Writers' Rain*, an anthology of pieces about the weather edited by Geoffrey Grigson – my pyjamas, sponge-bag and address book. Whenever I see that first-rate portrait of old man Garrick hanging from the wall, I ruminate as to his place on the English stage – mid-centre, centre-back, right half or wing three-quarter? How does one compare the numinous talents of Kean, Beerbohm Tree and Garrick, now that time – 'th'impassioned beggar' – has carried them from us? Which actor was the greatest Hamlet? I raised this very question at dinner here last night, but the actors on my table – Donny Sinden, Dickie Jacobi, Johnnie Gielgud and Larry Olivier – all of them far too modest to mention themselves – met the question with a wall of silence. Actors! I will be At Home at The Garrick for the next week or two, until I find a suitable *pied à terre* wherein to rest my weary bones. Letters eagerly received!

You gave felicitous mention to *Language, Truth and Logic* by my old chum Jack Ayer, who wrote it when he was barely out of shorts. He's well out of shorts now – though rarely out of doubles(!) – but can nevertheless hold his own whenever two or more logical positivists are gathered together. I once asked the old fighter if he had listed the Famous Three in order of preference, since they weren't by any stretch of the imagination in alphabetical order. 'If I reply "No" you will doubt my truth, if I reply "Yes" you will doubt my logic and if I reply "Maybe" you will doubt my language' he quipped, 'How's your glass?' My own personal favourite is language, for the daily miracles it performs, translucent, luminous, lucid, lucy, locketts. I love it for its welcome, its soup-on-the-boil, slippers-in-the-oven, abide-with-me *bonhomie* I love it for its devil-may-care, devil-take-the-hindmost, devilled kidneys, no-holds-barred effrontery. I love it for giving Shakespeare his poetry, Solzhenitsyn his weapon and Henry Miller his tool, for deceiving the believers and receiving the deliveries, for its passion, compassion and decompression, for its quiet nooks and vast open spaces. I love language for making possible the work of Susan Hill. [1]

Forgive these reveries, dear G. – I have had a perfectly maddening day on the Weidenfeld letters. Buoyed up by the bumper crop of politicoes willing to bop him a brief budget, Tubby is now dead set on raking in a member of

---

[1] Author and critic. Her five novel trilogy, *God, Things Are Awful* was described by Hermione Lee as 'a devastating indictment of happiness' whilst her later *My Jolly Cabbage Patch* was described by Claire Tomalin as 'a sensitive evocation of evocative sensitivity'.

the Royal Family, but I can't really see any of them playing ball. He says he has met the Queen a couple of times, and the last time – after his Investiture – they got on so well that she accepted a couple of his firm's books on what G.W. describes as 'very attractive terms – virtually a giveaway.' I still find it h. unlikely that she will put p. to p. I have told G.W. that the best we can hope for in that line is the most minimal memo plus signed photo from Princess Michael of Kent, and then only in return for a night out at Stringfellows with taxi home. He is displeased and insists Princess Margaret is a walkover.

I cannot enumerate too diligently the bits to which we are thrilled viz. your suggestions for Ken Crabbe's next *œuvre*. Ken went overboard for 'To Lacedaemon Did My Land Extend', so much so that he is changing the setting from Chippenham to Lacedaemon – a double bullseye for you, as it now becomes an historical novel, which has the marketing boys jumping for joy.

So glad you took to the Death book. Quite frankly, the problem is this: if we go ahead with it, the only bunch who will fall over backwards for it are the Elderly, and as a target group they are notoriously tight-fisted. Dr Johnson again: 'It is not the young who die first: it is the old; only when the young have become old do they die.' Top hole, surely?

Yours ever,
Harvey

My dear Harvey,

Your missives, willy-nilly the high-point of my week, reached an hypotheosis in the six-sider which rocketed through my letter box not eight days ago. My dear Harvey, you have always had the most remarkable aptitude for mixing the profound with the enchanting, and you have quite literally surpassed yourself on the perennially interesting topic of writers' feet. Delightful! Your fascinating theory stands up (!!!!) to close scrutiny (bye the bye, you know, of course that the original Dr Scrutiny was detailed to keep an assiduous eye on the household accounts of the spendthrift King James II) with but one paradox in the ointment, namely old Loopy-Loo herself, the Blessed Virginia Woolf of that parish. I am not denying that her feet were large – differing accounts put them anywhere between $7\frac{1}{2}$ and 9, which for a female is considerable – but I would venture to sugg. that her writing was not of a similarly expansive stature. No amount of running around observing people and living the life of Riley could tip her the wink that Mr and Mrs Joe Booklover have had streams of consciousness up to here and now wish to set up house on the sleepy shores of the Isle of Good-Read. But then perhaps your strictures on foot-size apply to writers as a whole, regardless of whether their outpourings are up to scratch.

There is nothing I should like more than to spend a week in The Garrick, surely the most congenial watering-hole in the metrop. For you, dear H., the urbane nonchalance you wear as a neck-tie allows you to knock knees with the great actors, politicians and writers of the day without so much as turning an hair, but for a country mouse such as myself, the very idea of sweltering in the heat of the fuminations of the celebrated sends a *frisson* of pleasure nipping up and down my spine. The real stars for me, of course, were the Music Hall Greats, the men – and women, let us not forget – who could illuminate the darkest theatre with their merry japes and tuneful ditties. Bouncing Jack Solomon and His Squeaky Canary, Little Annie Plesant and Her Outsized Voice, Fattie Kirkby and His Vanishing Cakes, Johnnie 'Jacko' Jumper, Freddie Raphael and His Amazing Expanding Head…these were the stuff upon which my dreams were erected. These days few of them continue to brighten the corridors of The Garrick, and fewer still are alive, but you must have a veritable plethora of modern theatricals among your fellow members and I'm sure they keep you awake till the early hours with their abundant range of amusing voices and expressions, catchphrases, anecdotes, funny laughs, gags, stunts and reminiscences. My one golden rule upon meeting an actor is to grab him – metaphorically speaking – by the lapels and to ask him if he has ever met with an hilarious disaster on stage. They invariably have a priceless *gaffe* up their sleeve and are only too happy to spill the beans in the fullest possible detail. Enchanting!

I mention this *mélange* of memorabilia *au théâtre* not merely as an agreeable means of passing the time of day (though besides eating lemon curd on fishcakes with Dickie Henderson on the wireless I, personally, can think of *nothing* more hopelessly and deliciously agreeable than the aforementioned pursuit) but as a prelude, a preview, a *hors d'œuvre* offered to your good self before I poke my head around your highly-polished door and, with a cautious 'coo-ee' place a proposal in your in-tray. Far be it from me to lecture you, dear Harvey, on what doth and what doth not get snapped up by the thirsty bookbuyer, but of this I am sure: for as long as the name 'Fattie Kirkby' is alive on the Nation's lips, there will always be someone who wants to read of his exploits and those of his fellow entertainers. For this reason, the suggestion which I tentatively but resolutely lay on your lap is this: that you undertake to publish (with the promise, I can safely assure you, of umpteen jackpots for yourself when we 'reap where we have tilled' (Matt. 3,5)) the work that has been my secret labour for nigh on twelve years, and is now, in the 'smouldering embers of my days' (Bridges) at last complete, namely, *Pass The Fruitcake, Iris* – A Collection of Catchphrases and Gaffes from The Golden Age of Music Hall Assembled by Gerald Marsh, esq.!

I can imagine your dear face on reading this news, and, to be honest, I share your delight that I have been employing my retirement years to profit, and not simply to deliver busloads of infinitely complex grades to the inky efforts of ignorant children. And you, my dear Harvey, whose faithful correspondence has been like 'a lamp to guide me to my sojourn' must be the first to gain from my enterprise. I therefore propose that you lean on your legal Johnnies to draw me up a contract post haste so that we all know which legs we are standing on and thence to a rapid first printing of – what? – 50,000? – so that we are in time for the Christmas hullaballoo. I haven't enclosed my labour of love (and lolly!) as I have only one copy about my person (handwritten, I need hardly say – I share with John Knox an almost physical detestation of the typewriter!) and I would most dearly love to be there to cherish the chortles as you give it its first read. I have attempted to include a joke or witty *riposte* on every one of its 983 pages, so I feel preternaturally confident that you and Mr and Mrs Joe Bookbuyer will savour the more scholarly passages wherein are rendered the most popular music hall jokes of the 1890s in their closest possible Latin, Greek and Hebrew translations as much as you will the more obviously light-hearted profiles of one hundred and twenty of the most well-respected impresarios of the era. I imagine that you are beaming as you read this, and I modestly admit that Hyacinth would tell you that you have good reason: she has been reading the MS for over a year and has still not reached the end! I imagine you would like to set eyes on it as soon as poss., so perhaps it would be most wise if you were to send a minion in an automobile for it, but do remember to 'telephone' first, as I have recently taken to accompanying Hyacinth on her metal-detecting jaunts.

Your prose-poem, for it was surely that, to the varieties and vagaries of our English tongue was little short of delicious, and should be anthologised this minute. It calls to mind the story of the late and (inarguable, surely?) very great Winston Churchill who, confronted by a large and rather ugly female Socialist in the corridors at Westminster, said, 'Madam, we have, in this native land of ours, that most malleable of beasts, that most merciful mother, that most various of visitors, a language which is, by its very jot and grain, able to encompass all action in a mere handful of words, but, Madam…' and here, alas, I forget the exact verbiage W.

employed, but, suffice it to say, the female Socialist ended up flat on her back with a black eye, the great man merrily by-passing her, familiar cigar in mouth, smiling from ear to ear. Priceless!

The diligent researcher from 'Arts Aplenty!' has been making more noises in my direction. It appears that they wish to place me in front of the motion picture camera with a view to recording for posterity the full story of that rather sordid little incident we had to clear up when you were a pupil of mine in '48. I happened to mention it (I *do* hope that you regard it, as I do, as *eau sur le pont*) in a carefree moment on his last visit. Like you, I have a natural aversion to appearing on 'the small screen' – but I don't like to let the poor fellow down, so I have replied in the adjustable affirmative.

I *so* look forward to your reaction to *Pass the Fruitcake, Iris.*

Yours ever,
Gerald

23 May 1983   *Garrick Club*

My dear Gerald,

Re your spirited questioning of me over the purpose and House Rules of the EXIT club, as mentioned to your good self by our author chum from the Society of Jesus, I have been swatting up on all its whys and wherefores, and I must say I think it sounds just the thing for you. It has had a healthy following among the intellectual community, many of them 'seeing the light', as it were, shortly before their deaths, and though its members come and go, they tend to carry with them the reliable epithet, 'Once a member, always a member'. They are a branch of the 'Do-It-Yourself' movement which now seems to be sweeping (why is it always *sweeping*, never dusting, spring-cleaning or polishing?) the country, but without the awful 'elbow grease' connotations that term generally calls to mind – the late Arthur Koestler (what a mind!) was dead keen, *par exemple*.

I am eternally grateful to you for the generosity of spirit and, as I have always said, extraordinary latitude of mind which have provided me with the unsettling paradox of Virginia Woolf and her feet. This will prove quite a teaser for the Paedophile Soc. when I address it next week, and raises the whole question of whether or not the wearisome writer was in fact male, a problem I will bring up in a paper to the August meeting of The Holroyd Group, under the title, 'Virginia – Man or Woolf?' I'm abundantly confident that this will raise the temperature of debate up to the standard of that hardy annual – 'Was Shakespeare Bacon?' (one of my favourite opening quips when addressing high-powered literati on this puzzle is, 'You'd better ask his butcher – he'll tell you that he was definitely no chicken but may well have been game(!!!!!)' – I find it induces merriment in even the most dour post-Structuralist) and already the most dedicated Woolfians and collectors of Woolfiana are closing ranks.

My dear Gerald, life *au* Garrick is not the hurly-burly of fun and games you crack it up to be, I can assure you. Most of the members are ordinary mortals who like nothing better than to put their feet up after a hard day's slog and though they are easily avoided it is these quite normal blokes who make up the backbone of the building. There are those who lionize the well-known, as I was saying to Jimmy Tarbuck only the other night, but they are quite easily dealt with by calling Cyril Fletcher over into the group. No, dear G., my life here is taken up with the tedious *minutiae* of publishing – the 'editing' of G.W.'s letters (breathe not a word abroad, but Princess Michael of K. has come up trumps, delivering by return of p. over 300 words on 'Stars This Royal Highness Has Met' – they include Lord Matthews, Pat Phoenix and Angela Rippon – and all for the price of a large rum and coke and tickets for two to 'Singin' in the Rain' at the Adelphi), the preparation of my Writers and Their Feet paper, the day-to-day admin. of the Worshipful Company of Authors (I have nabbed Jonathan Raban to deliver the Susan Hill Memorial Lecture on 'Rows I have Enjoyed – A Seafarer Recollects') and the seemingly never-ending interviews I am duty bound to spout for 'Arts Aplenty!'. This brings me to the somewhat delicate matter of your own involvement in the increasingly silly prog. The last thing I wish to do, my dearest Gerald, is deprive you of your last hope of National and International Gogglebox Stardom (though if David Frost can 'make it' I see no reason why you shouldn't!!!) but I do feel that the recounting of that – as you put it – 'rather sordid little incident' *ad infinitum* would, I must stress too strongly, severely jeopardise those quite faultless and noble institutions with which I am associated – the WCA, Amnesty International, the Publisher's Circle, The Arts Council, The Garrick, *Who's Who*, the OEA, The Mentally Handicapped Publishers Association and, in no small way, my own company. May I suggest (wasn't it Joseph Stalin of that Ilk who always prefaced his commands with 'may I suggest…'?) that you put the dampeners on that particular anecdote (which would doubtless be considered anyway too trifling to squeeze into the final 'cut') and instead regale Mr and Mrs Joe Tellyholic with your delicious rendering of my (somewhat disastrous!) performance in the House stab at *Samson Agonistes*?

This would afford you ample opportunity for showing the world and his wife your quite splendid array of funny voices, and – strictly between these four walls – I happen to know that the producer of 'Call My Bluff' is casting a blind eye around for an 'unknown' (trade parlance for a still-to-be-discovered 'personality') who has impish impersonations on the very tip of his tongue. I leave it to you.

I am unequivocally thrilled that it is me on whom you have chosen to off-load your long-secreted *Meisterwerk*. You have obviously derived a lot of satisfaction from the task you set yourself, a task which anyone else would have abandoned long ago. This mammoth and – of this I have no doubt – informative book will, I feel sure, in future years become the standard textbook for all those whose direct concern is the history of the catchphrases and gaffes of the golden age of Music Hall. You and your subject will be forever associated as you walk hand in hand together down the steadily darkening corridors of history. *Do* let me see the MS at the earliest possible opportunity, my dear G., though I think it would be safer (and, by Jove, a good sight more historic!) if I were to pick it up personally from your own much-treasured hands, rather than let some guttersnipe clamp his grubby mitts on it, with all the ensuing dangers that grim spectacle would entail. Herein lies the nub of a minor problem: what with one thing and another (and another, and another, and another – as Bert Ford once said, it never comes down in scattered showers but it brings in an heavy anti-cyclone from the West!) I have been unable to lay my hands on an up-to-date British Railways timetable, and this, combined with imminent, and, in my view highly sensible, cuts *à la* Beeching, suggests to me that I should delay my longed for trip until "aft the sails be hoisted'. If I remember rightly, T.E. Lawrence, he of Arabia, spent eight years slaving away on *Seven Pillars of Wisdom* before losing it on Reading Station. But, my dear soul, I can't tell you how I am already experiencing the 'sweet anticipation of the fever'd brow' in my near-delirious anticipation of first setting eyes on your time-honoured gem.

Your mention of Winston sets my mind whirring over this puzzle: who are the great men of today? I'm sure *you* have some up your sleeve!

Yours ever,
Harvey

My dear Harvey,

My chair is fair a-wobble as I jump for joy at the supremely felicitous news of your rapturous reception of my humble offering to the world of literature. I am so glad that I am now empowered to repay you for the immense pleasure our correspondence has given me, week in, week out, and that 'happy days are here again' for your firm. You ask what kept me going 'come rain or shine' through those twelve years of toil. It was this. Ever since the age of, what, three or four, I have derived sublime satisfaction from settling into a comfortable armchair with one of the World's Minor Masterpieces then, very slowly, for haste hath no place in the begetting of wisdom, running my fingers over its covers, gently imbibing its texture. My long-cherished routine is then to hold the Classic in both hands, lifting it, in one long and exceedingly gradual movement, to my nostrils, which, at a given command, commence a careful and joyous inhalation, savouring each whiff and morsel of its very *paperiness*; after many minutes of sniffing, I replace the beloved book in the nub of my lap and, employing one hand to keep it steady, with the other I riffle the pages, not noisily, not violently, but quietly and smoothly, so that the congenial flip-flap of leaf upon leaf fills my mind with 'the tranquil remembrance of things to come' and I can bathe freely in the soft purr of Literature pouring forth upon itself; as this pleasure luxuriously subsides I prepare myself for the apogee of my journey into the very centre of the printed adventure: I position the firmly closed book, face up, on the top of my legs, two inches from my bended knee, taking much care to manoeuvre its edges so that it lies there full square in its deep majesty, and then, at last, I let my eyes skip and dance over its cover, rejoicing in the colour and grain of its cloth and the simplicity or elaboration of its lettering if that cover be plain, in the depiction of person or persons in the landscape or interior if that cover be illustrated; then, and only then, having basked contentedly in the warm pools and gushing waterfalls of World Literature, do I return the volume to its place on the shelf, snug in the conjecture that one day it will be there to be read at my leisure. And after so many, many years of eliciting so much pleasure from books, I was determined to give something in return, and that is why I kept up the hard slog for those long, and, yes, it must be admitted, occasionally lonely, twelve years. Pah! But I ramble. Let it suffice to tell you that I am quite literally tickled pink by your transparent enthusiasm, and I can assure you it will be repaid plentifold.

Alack and alas, as that tedious old harridan Mrs Macbeth would say, I fairly draw a blank to your most perceptive and pertinent interrogative *re* wither the Great Men. Three cheers for Mrs T., *mais oui!* but the rest of the party strike one as a trifle shoddy, *eh bien?* On the Opposition benches, Roy Hattersley is quite evidently a Great Writer (did you by any chance catch his splendid piece on how coming to terms with acne turned him into a life-long Socialist?) but does this, *quo vadis*, mean that he is also a Great Man? Time alone (though perhaps with an elbow from his close chum Freddy Fate) will tell.

I have long been drawn by those who argue that V.

Woolf was a man. I was first prompted to this theory –
for it *is* still a theory – by the footnote on page 693 of
Volume Two (*The Doldrum Years*) of Quentin Bell's
endlessly learned biog. of the scrawny scrivener, wherein
he mentions *en passant* that between paragraphs she was
wont to take five good, strong puffs on the pipe given her
by her father. This most tenuous of clues led me to read
for the first time at least one of her novels, *Orlando* (later
made into a telly series with Sam Kydd in the title role)
and the photograph on the jacket (why 'jacket', I
wonder? wouldn't overcoat, gown or, most elegant of all,
robe fit better?) seemed to this amateur literary sleuth to
set the icing on the cake and the cat among the pigeons.
There, on the mantelpiece in the background, beyond
the profile of Virginia looking for all the world as if she'd
just burnt the fishfingers, was the hazy but unmistakable
silhouette of a bowler hat. A year or maybe more later I
read the following on page 352 in Volume 9 of her
Collected Postcards: 'L. has made off with my bowler &
with my corduroys & he knows I cannot write without
them & I have taken to bed with a fever & you must
remember that I have loved you more dearly than I ever
thought possible & two pints today please milkman & no
cream. V.' Game, set and match, methinks.

I must stop writing now, as I will already be in
Hyacinth's black books for playing truant from my duties
as Assistant to the Metal Detector, an *ex officio* post
which involves muddying one's digits at the first hint of a
bleep from that over-sensitive contraption. Anagrams
have had to take a back seat to this most recent of H's
enthusiasms, though once in bed, Origami permitting,
she allows herself a lean fifteen minutes to resume work
on this year's long-term project – an anagram of

'Baroness Orczy', her best effort thus far being 'Xylophone .

I can't tell you how perfectly fascinated I was to glimpse the distress that the prospect of my retelling of that old chestnut you term 'that rather sordid little incident' so obviously causes your heart. My dear old thing, bygones are surely bygones, and all the more worthy of resurrection for that, you must surely agree. Of course, my dear H., I will let you twist my arm, but as this is an action that can only be performed 'in person' I suggest you whizz over to Bookends as soon as is humanly poss. and we can have a high old time pulling legs, twisting arms, sticking our necks out and – yes, why not, after all? – putting our feet in it. The garden is a melodious aquarium of fragrant tints and my 'garden shed' (!!!) is well-stocked with bottles, tubs and tubes and should that array prove insufficient I have managed to secure a medium-dry household bleach, so you will not leave our little haven thirsty, I can assure you!

Yours ever,
Gerald

P.S. Your presence *chez* Bookends will be doubly agreeable for you, as I will be able to hand you over my *magnum opus* and you will no longer have to endure the torture of a prolonged dawdle. Capital! G.

10 June 1983   *The Garrick*

My dear Gerald,

I am greatly enamoured of your gorgeous invitation to partake of a stay in the country, and accept with alacrity. No doubt we will have even more fun than Lady Chatterley (or 'Lady Chatterbox' as Jack Perelman once called her!) ensconced in the potting-shed, though I daresay our tumblers will be of a less energetic inclination than her Ladyship's! I trust you will excuse me if I stay in London a couple of ticks longer; I have a number of loose ends to tie up (Tubby W., like a bull in a sweetshop, now wishes for a correspondence with not only Henry Kissinger and Frankie Vaughan but President Sadat as well; whenever I inform him that the latter is as dead as a dodo he snaps back that Rome wasn't built in a day) and would like to leave things shipshape afore setting sail for foreign climes. How glorious sounds your garden! Was it not the late, great William Cobbett who first observed that a garden with neither shrubs nor flowers is like a carpark without automobiles? Succulent image!

What an odd lot the Paedophiles turned out to be! Not at all the grey, earnest demurely-dressed shower I had been expecting. Not a bit of it. Most of them were dressed any-old-how, in shirts with bright stripes or spots or both, some of them open-necked but the majority cravatted. Their trousers were coloured in weird shades of russet and green; their shoes, which one might have expected to have been exclusively of the highest quality material, with perhaps the uncomfortable look of the foot-conscious, were suede to a man. Their jackets had belts dangling from the side. A rum bunch, wholly male I might add, and though they obviously blended into the background at The Garrick, they would have looked quite a sight anywhere else. My paper was politely received, but there was curiously little consternation over our V. Woolf hypothesis and barely a mutter at some of my wilder conjectures *re* the probable size of the Wellingtons Tolstoy wore. In point of fact, the only question put to me (by the Secretary himself) after a hushed silence at the end of my talk was, 'Exactly how old was Ginny Woolf?' Following what I considered to be a decidedly tepid vote of thanks from Master Chairman, during which he was at least (how one clutches at the dampest straws!) kind enough to create me an Honorary Member, the meeting adjourned to 'Playland', which they informed me was an arcade. They encouraged me to hop along with them, insisting with a peculiar glee that they would be 'just looking'. No doubt their idea of earthly Paradise is the observation of shoppers' feet as they march up and down an arcade, but it most certainly isn't mine, so I made my excuses.

I must now turn to Camelia. She is, as you know, a woman; and neither better nor worse for that. But the obvious physical difference between the two of us is, alas, not the only point on which we part company. She is something of a health fanatic and has always taken what I in my pettish way have tended to consider a disproportional interest in her own body and those of others. She says that I am owlish, and I daresay there is something in that, though I would prefer the adjective bookish myself. And it is books, dear, innocent things that they are, which have been our undoing. Whilst I would regard my leather-bound 12 volume editions of

Socrates' *Principia Mathematica* or Pater's *Emissio Nocturna* as works of incalculable wisdom, beauty and – yes – sustenance, Camelia looks upon them solely as apparati for keeping her body 'in trim' (ghastly, female phrase). Even now I wince at the memory of the time I ambulated into the library to discover Camelia with a *Lyrical Ballads* First Edition in her hands and at her feet the Folio Society's handsome edition of *Five Go Shrimping Again* with an introduction by Dora Russell. A laudable sight, you might hastily conclude, but *au contraire*! – Camelia was employing the Blyton as a toe expander and she was attempting to tear the Lyrical B.'s in two 'as a test of willpower'. She regularly weightlifts with Socrates and Walter Pater. We had, I suppose, been drifting apart for many calendar months, both in the physical sense – Camelia's tent and bivouac have become permanent fixtures on our croquet lawn – and in the mental sense – she would only speak to me once a week, while I was straining to listen to 'Critics Forum' on the estimable Radio Three. Our marriage, then, was not all that it might have been and had lost some of its original vigour: no more the shared love of 'Knock Knock' jokes (irresistible, surely?), no more plumping up the cushions together at the end of a busy day, no more whistling duets from the repertoire of The Kings Singers during washing-up time, no more painting of each other's toenails. Where before we had revelled in Pelmanism, now we toyed at patience; games of Monopoly would disintegrate over our disparate interpretations of Free Parking; piggyback rides had long ceased after C.'s somewhat tetchy complaints of cricks in her back. Despite these impedimenta we might have bumbled along quite merrily, our knapsack choc-a-bloc with petty upsets but our walking shoes stout enough to take the weight. Wasn't it Oscar who said 'There is nothing more delightful than a schism. It draws people together so'? For a time, we might have believed him but when 'Neil' the New Zealander (decry me as prejudiced if you will, but has *any* Great – or even medium-Great – work of literature emanated from that silly little country? I think not) entered stage left, I began to perceive hiccoughs in our day-to-day life that in turn led me to the frankly painful realisation that Camelia's attention was turned towards another, and that was far from being me. It was when I returned from a hard day's work to find my library converted into what Neil delighted in designating a 'work-out space', replete with my emptied shelves acting as climbing rails, my goatskin Walter Scott as an horse and my precious *Collected John Bunyan* as an assault course that I made my first, and last, attempt to blow the whistle on things. 'What about my Bunyan?' I yelled at Neil, whose beads of sweat were discolouring the vellum of *P.'s Progress*. 'If you did a bit more exercise, you wouldn't have one,' he replied, his Antipodean grin never faltering for a second. No more pettifogging ninnies for me, I thought, and off I popped to The Garrick, which is willy-nilly more central. I would have let you know of this position sooner, but I did not want to disturb your enjoyment of Wimbledon week.

How I *long* to be with you within the fortnight, dipping in and out of your eminently publishable manuscript and rehearsing you through that *Samson Agonistes* gag.

Yours ever,
Harvey

P.S. Something for your 'little grey cells' to ponder. I have this morning received a brief missive from the Chairman of the National Book League begging my presence on a panel to select the 20 Funniest Books of All Time. My fellow judges would be Sir Peter Parker and Tim Rice, so I found the invitation irresistible. And just when I was struggling to find time to plod through a book I *really wanted to read*...H.

21 June 1983   *Bookends*

My dear Harvey,

You should know, my dear Harvey, that nothing but nothing would disturb my enjoyment of Wimbledon week, though I feel not a little fidgety when the totally unlettered John McEnroe starts poking fun (and worse!) at the shortsightedness of the elderly referees. How very disappointing for you must be the thought of your Camelia hobnobbing with a marsupial, but I daresay you will take to bachelorhood like a d. to w. and within a week or two you will have forgotten that you had ever been spliced. *Strictly* between you, me and the postman, on the odd occasion on which I am free from my dearest H. – her annual week in Stockton to see her much-loved motorbike scrambling, say, or her visits to her sister Elspeth at Parkhurst – I find much to savour in her absence. Instead of Scrabble, I run my fingers over books (one can get through over fifty in the time); instead of metal detecting, I chew soap (an habit acquired at school and never ditched), and rather than get up in the morning I stay in bed, eating my meals (mainly from cans, I fear) straight off the sheets, so there's none of that nonsense with dirty plates, etcetera. Chin up, old chum, there are many worse things than losing one's wife – the enforced reading of a novel by Dorothy Richardson, *par exemple* (!).

My natural sense of mischief seems to be playing havoc with my innate sense of justice, *mayor cooper*. Hyacinth, doughty metal hunter that she is, has raked in a small fortune (whisper it quietly in the glades, but it whistles to the tune of a none-too-modest £44,000). Never having been a contraption man myself, I find it impossible to furnish you with a description of how her machine, skilfully handled by H. (with expert assistance from yours t.!) managed to pre-condition the sub-waves, decipher the electro-magnetic forces, reassemble the active modules, or whatever – oh, for a purge on jargon! – but I can inform you in fine old layman's terms, honed by the centuries, that one minute the two of us were prospecting in the rain – H. in charge with sou'wester and contraption, little m. trailing with *Sunday Telegraph* on head (incidentally, did you catch Peregrine Worsthorne's splendid article forcefully arguing for repatriation of the Belgians?) and sieve in hand – and the next minute the blessed thing was making the most shameless (but to H.'s trained ears, felicitous) high-pitched wail. Whenever Hyacinth gets over-excited, her stockings ladder, and I can tell you as God (present, I wonder?) is my witness that on our return home they looked as if they'd been used for rifle practice. But I skip: as, indeed, we both did when we discovered what we had unearthed, a mere two inches under ground. At first, it looked like one of those tins in which are housed what I believe are known as 'baked beans'. But lo! one dab from Hyacinth's ever-present Quickies and the unmistakable glow of gold found us screwing up our eyes. We had come across a 2,000-year-old goblet made of solid gold; a remnant, experts later informed us, of an Aztec 'splinter group' which had settled briefly in Herefordshire *circa* 30 BC but which had soon moved on, owing to language difficulties. Within seconds of her discovery, Hyacinth had decided that she had no wish to sit on it and, barely drawing breath for a cup of blackcurrant Ovaltine *chez*

Bookends, she leapt onto the speediest locomotive Herefordshire offers, arriving at an excited Sotheby's just prior to house lock-up time. The egg-heads at S's were agog, offering H. a choice of chairs and any number of soft (and some not-so-soft!) drinks. Bob's your uncle, our 'little gleamer', as H. insists on terming it, comes up for auction next week, with a reserve of £44,000. Hyacinth has, quite right and properly, made it crystal clear that as unemployed sieve-carrier, my own role in the find merits little share of the booty (hear, hear) but she promises me a particularly bulging stocking come Christmas. She further insists that her windfall will not change her in any way (boast or threat? I jest, of course).

Never has your literary judgement been more perfectly sharp than in your summary of the New Zealand literary scene (or rather lack of!!!). Throwing caution to the wind, I would venture that not only has no work of literature, great, medium-great, classic, minor-classic, masterpiece, neglected masterpiece, flawed masterpiece, unfinished miniature, important landmark, vital contribution to the *genre*, indispensable forerunner, or even vivid portrayal *come out* of New Zealand, but I doubt whether any has ever even got into that God-forsaken outpost. Was Lillian Hellman a Maori? I would hazard a guess that she was not. Likewise Ngaio Marsh (anagram: Michelangelo). I believe Robert Morley once did a 'promotional' tour of the said country, but he is a writer of lesser stature than, say, Arnold Bennet or Louisa M. Alcott, neither of whom gave it a second thought. It would seem that on the literary front, you beat friend Neil hands down.

Who is Mr (presumably) Tim Rice? In my day, only cats were called 'Tim', and then only in fun, but now the woods are awash with them. But for Sir Peter Parker I have the greatest respect – I believe he can quote from Blake – and I can well see why you accepted the summons to join his court with such alacrity. The 20 Funniest Books of All Time presents quite a poser, does it not? I found Alan Coren's last volume of *Collected Pieces June 16th 1982-July 25th 1982* highly amusing, particularly his (intentional) mistaking of Norman Tebbit for the Minister of Employment. Priceless! But perhaps such collections are inadmissible; if so I would submit a book called *Deep Throat* by a young lady writer called Linda Lovelace. Do give it a go: it's a sort of female Billy Bunter set in New York with a girl who is forever reduced to grunts and groans as a consequence of trying to speak with her mouth full, well up to the demanding standard set by Frank Richards. Our old favourite, Susan Hill, has written a tremendously witty novel called *The Magic Apple Tree* in which the hilariously absurd heroine, writing in the first person, is convinced that she is the first person ever to have lived in the countryside and gets into some marvellous tight spots enthusing over an apple, the grass, the sun *etcetera*: a parody, but none the worse for that. These three books are well worth a dip, along with anything of Denis Norden you can get your hands on.

Mr Dainty, the diligent researcher, availed himself of Mr Bell's invention in order to book an appointment for filming my 'piece' about you. I delayed my television *début* until after your State Visit to Bookends. Not wishing to leave him 'empty-handed' as it were, I tipped him the wink about your new Honorary Membership of the Paedophile Society, and I can't tell you how his ears pricked up: it is evidently a more notable institution than your (quite brilliant, I might add) impressions of its individual members suggest. But then was it not Elizabeth David who first noted that a slice of bread is only the sum total of its crumbs?

So *very much* looking forward to your visit. Is that splendid mouth organ still in your possession? *Do* bring it if it is – Hyacinth falls over backwards for a sing-song.

Yours ever,
Gerald

28 June 1983   *The Garrick Club*

My dear Gerald,

Knowing the efficiency of Her Majesty's Postal Service, it seems well within the realms of possibility that when you read this budget at your breakfast table you will be able to look up over your packet of All Bran and espy Yours t. seated opposite you, quivering in trepidation lest his grammar doth not uphold. But let us act on the assumption that such an *folie de grandeur* will not take place and that you will have a full day to inwardly digest my paltry musings afore their perpetrator puts his foot through the doorway.

Dear, dear Hyacinth must, like that most restless of cows, be 'over the moon' at the little pot of gold that has winged its way over the rainbow and into her lap. I am quite ravenous to plant a congratulatory kiss on her fair cheek in person, but until that merry moment arrives would you be so good as to convey my heartiest and let her know that I am composing a number of congratulatory anagrams for her even as I write. I have also been brushing up on my Scrabble, so that you, dear G., will be able to enjoy a well-earned rest in your library whilst H. and I battle it out for the Triple Word Scores.

Many thanks for your w.'s of w. *re* my newfangled bachelor status. There are, as you intimated, a number of advantages allotted to those whose wives have Gone East. I can now watch the television (monstrous invention) sitting down, whereas before C. insisted that we stand, proclaiming it good for the digestion or some such cobblers. I can fall soundly into the land of Nod within seconds of skull touching feathers without the bi-weekly scare that C. will start treating me as a cross between a whippet and a trampolene. Furthermore, I can read in bed *au matin* without her ripping out the endpapers when her wretched *papier mâché* figurines start to go to the dogs. Restaurant bills are cut in half, and there is no need to yap. Entertaining literary friends, I can mention the names of, say, Conrad, Dostoievsky and Thackeray without a shrill voice piping in, 'Who's he when he's at home?' I can listen to my beloved Radio Three in the morning without the inevitable, 'Terry sounds a little glum today, doesn't he?' Yes, the benefits are multitudinous. I think it was Kahlil Karmen who said, 'You are never truly alone unless you are by yourself' and I am beginning to experience the devastating yet paradoxically joyful truth behind that rich advice.

Of course, there are things about Camelia that I shall never forget: her ability to keep two ferrets simultaneously down her trousers for over three-and-a-half hours; her love of blood sports, her support of capital punishment, and her unflinching hope that one day the two could be combined; her use of ammonia bleach as a mouth wash; her extraordinary competence as an arm wrestler; her hair, both on and off; her Commonplace Book, filled to bursting with snaps of Roger Whittaker; her immense generosity to others (though rarely to me); and her overriding belief that in an earlier life she had been Captain W. E. Johns.

But beneath the façade there is often pain, a truth first sighted by Henrik Ibsen as he cast his beady eye among the *fjords*, and later by Tennessee Williams on the banks of the Mississippi. Of course, neither of those estimable playwrights came up with any solutions, but then they were in no position to avail themselves of the deep leather seats of The Garrick, where cigar smoke is as nectar to the bee, and where the dying art of conversation has come to make its peace.

But I ramble. The Weidenfeld letters are very nearly 'in the bag', though G.W. is anxious to read them before they are published and he now thinks it unlikely that he will be able to find the time for another two months. Even though I penned five missives to Henry Kissinger, on a veritable cornucopia of subjects from the situation in South America to his impressions of Michael Parkinson, he was resolutely unforthcoming, failing even to acknowledge their safe arrival.

Glum looks from Tubby, then, until I hit upon the idea of roping in *another* Henry Kissinger, and, as luck would have it, after a rummage or two in the regional telephone directories I located an Henry Kissinger who was – and, I might add, still is – the Catering Manager at the Berni Inn at Tavistock; a charming man, only too willing to reply to any letter we sent him, and all for the price of a slap-up meal for four at the local Schooner Inn. Though his views on bits and bobs were a little off t'other Kissinger's beaten track – he dislikes all Americans, lock, stock and barrel (excluding one Telly Savalas, on whom he dotes), he reckons God was an astronaut and he is under the illusion that Cambodia is something you put in the bath to make it frothy – only the most nit-picking so-called 'expert' could detect the discrepancies, so chocks away.

Multitudinous thanks for up-backing me on the New Z. issue. I have already rushed off a p.c. to Camelia pointing out her new friend's cultural vacuity, though knowing her she will see this as the most risible of objections and brush it firmly to one side. Pity the uncultured, as Walpole once said, for without culture no man can be truly cultured. My gratitude also rains down on you, dear G., for providing me with such useful suggestions to take with me to the Funny Books panel – the Susan Hill had the tears literally rolling into the armagnac, the Lovelace I have been unable to get my hands on, but sounds a hoot, and as for Coren – well, the three of us are confidently expecting that at least five of his books will nudge their way into the final Top Twenty.

Sir Peter P. goes great guns for *Three Men in a Boat* though I suspect his choice has a business bias, for what book could more surely turn the reader towards the safety and comfort of the train (!!!) and he maintains that much of Blake is gorgeously witty, a case he went a long way towards proving by his rendering of 'Tiger, Tiger, Burning Bright' in the (rather exaggerated) accent of a Cornish yokel. Tim Rice (who is Tim Rice, indeed! my dear Gerald, have you, in your rustic isolation, really not heard of the musical 'Cats'?) maintains that Jesus Christ had a great sense of humour and that if he were alive today he would undoubtedly be a lyricist for a West End musical *pace* the Parables and much of the Sermon on the Mount, but P.P. and my good self maintain that it is against the rules to divide up a book, and taken as a whole the New Testament is *not* a funny book (and nor was it meant to be). The Great Debate continues in a fortnight, by which time I am duty bound to have read through Arianna Stassinopoulos's book, *Maria Callas*.

I will be arriving at Nookey Rest station at 11.27 on

Saturday morning, my bag o'erflowing with gifts for both of you, my mind o'erflowing with anagrams of a literary bent for Hyacinth, and my expectation o'erflowing with thoughts of *Pass the Fruitcake, Iris.*

Yours e'er till then,
Harvey

My dear Gerald,[1]

This is a hard letter to pen, but I know that our friendship, which has, after all, owed its very existence to the written word, will not balk at anything simply because it is *un peu difficile*. I think it was W.S. Gilbert (irascible old rogue!) who first coined the phrase 'A friend in need is a friend indeed', and since you are now in need, I do trust you will count me as your dearest friend.

I have deposited this missive beside the tumbler containing your teeth, as my dear Hyacinth informs me that this is your first port of call upon awakening each day, and we are both keen that you should be the first to know of our departure from 'Bookends' together at daybreak. Neither of us wished to call a halt to your sweet slumbers (your snores, I might add, called to mind Poe's 'Wildbeestes of Cracow, cantankerous in dreams'), so after a hastily snatched breakfast (I do hope you don't mind – I pilfered the plastic panda from the All-Bran as a small gift for H.) we have tiptoed away to, as I. Fleming would have put it, 'destinations unknown'. H. has just this minute asked me to tell you that the jelly moulds are adjacent to the catfood should you be peckish for your favourite pud.

As neither one of us (thank goodness for like minds!) is overfond of the romantic scribblers, I will spare you

[1] *Editor's note*: One of two letters in the correspondence to have been hand-delivered. It seems likely that G.M. read it immediately upon awakening.

both the Cartlands and the Lawrences in the description which I think I owe you of the whys and wherefores of the coming together (and leaving together!!!) of Hyacinth, your wife and myself (that sounds like three people, but is, of course, only two, as Hyacinth is – or at very least was (!) your wife). First, I must heartily assure you that Hyacinth's recent jackpot is nothing compared to the genuine love I feel for her – she has a heart of gold and a *joie de vivre* I value above all else. No, I think we were first drawn together by our shared love of the alphabet, that oilfield of letters, both consonants and vowels, which, when tapped, provides the fuel for all words, sentences and paragraphs. Whilst you sat in the next-door room chewing your soap and fingering your leather-bounds, Hyacinth and I played game upon game of Scrabble, and as each word took its place on the board, we would discuss it, be it short (it, bin, ox) or long (idea, bite, bins). Did we enjoy it *as a word* or were we to some extent influenced by its earthly connotations? Could we find an anagram (bin becomes nib, ox becomes xo)? Might we be able to compose a sentence, however ridiculous the meaning, from the words on show (Bins ox it, idea: bite bin!)? These were the sort of linguistic problems which conspired to become our joint obsession, and as we beavered away in this common pursuit we began to realise that our true love was not words, or even Scrabble, but each other. Hyacinth has just asked me to remind you not to forget to feed Mr Pickwick, and could you please cancel her subscription to *Psychic News*? From talking about words, we began to move on to talking about ourselves, our hopes and our dreams. Hyacinth told me that her dream was to spend her newly acquired fortune on someone who would appreciate it. You will be glad to hear, my dear G., that at this juncture I put your name forward as a candidate, but no, she was adamant that your happiness lay in glue, soap and books and that to lure you away from the simple things of life would be like offering a red rag to a bull. Hyacinth then turned her gaze to me, and through those entrancing bifocals of hers she whispered, 'It is you on whom my choice has fallen, dear Harvey. I will share my fortune with none other'. She then added, 'Should it be "on whom" or "on who"?' ' "On Whom" ' I replied, 'Though I am dissatisfied with "none other". In the circumstances, "no other" would be preferable.' We sat arguing the toss for quite a while, but the full implications of what Hyacinth had suggested stayed 'lingering in the murmurs of the mind'. This was on the first night of my stay, and no more such intimate words passed between Hyacinth and myself for the rest of the evening, partly, as you remember, due to your recitation after dinner of comic monologues from the late 1880s as a 'taster' for your book, and partly due to Hyacinth's natural reticence: as you know, she hides behind her Origami whenever a decision looms.

That night, my sleep was disagreeably slow in arriving. I remember hearing the floorboards creak and rumble as H. went about both her one o'clock and four thirty goldfish feeding stints. Of Hyacinth I was sure – my love was complete and unchequed; but how would this appear to you, my dear G. that was the question which preyed upon my brow 'twixt the close of moonlight and the rising of the sun, would this be the end of a correspondence – and an eminently civilised correspondence at that – which might, thirty years hence shine like a beacon of light amongst the stranglehold of push-button communication which so beset the 1980s? Can love ever justify the termination of civilisation? The all-too-recent death of Lord Clark[1] made my soul-searching all the more solitary, all the more poignant.

The next day, which was only yesterday but now seems so very long ago, you and I spent much time together in the garden shed (what an excellent Bloody Mary you mix – wasn't it Winston himself who maintained that you could tell the cut of a man's gib by his prowess with the aforesaid B.M.?) but you seemed so wrapped up in your undoubtedly excellent manuscript that it seemed tactless to start throwing around questions as to whether or nay I should, as it were, nip off with your beloved spouse. Hyacinth has just asked me to ask you whether you would be so good as to tell Mary Killen that she will be unable to give her talk on The Post-Structuralist Movement in Paper-Folding but that the slides are already in the projector. And so our conversation rambled on, through the vicissitudes (marvellous word!) of whether either one of us would have cared to have been operated on by Dr Johnson, whether the man from Porlock didn't arrive a moment too soon and whether the Church of England isn't getting a little over-excited by something that happened yonks ago, and Abroad of all places! In the interval between each of these most agreeable *divertissements* you entertained me with more readings from *Pass The Fruitcake, Iris,* and apart from one or two quibbles over size, style and content I confirmed that I would be more than delighted to run it through our presses. (Incidentally, I have taken the MS

---

[1] Art Historian. His catchphrase 'Let us now pass onto the next room' took on undertones of additional poignancy after his death in 1983.

with me *aux vacances* for further perusal – I promise not to lose it down the waste-disposal!!!) Throughout this eminently delicious day I found myself with little desire to take a pin to your reveries, so I remained as twinkling and affable as I felt. A divine Sunday was rounded off by your excellent recounting of my *faux pas* in S. Agonistes (to me he has always sounded suspiciously like a second-hand car dealer!), though if I were you I would avoid mentioning the incident backstage with the lipstick – it would be adjudged by the prod. what is technically known as 'bad television'.

I hope, my dear Gerald, that these few lines go some way towards explaining why Hyacinth and I are nowhere to be found on this Monday morning, and I trust that it has dispelled any anachronistic notions of hard f.s from your side of the fence.

If you could post your next missive care of The Garrick, I'm sure their trusty servants will 'forward' it; needless to say, we are both dying to hear from you.

Yours ever,
Harvey

P.S. What are your five favourite words for rolling around your mouth?

P.P.S. And your five least favourite?

P.P.P.S. Don't you find Tony Powell's spelling exemplary throughout his immortal *Music of T.* series (still read today, I wonder?). Hyacinth has just asked me to tell you not to confuse the catfood with the jelly.

My dear Harvey,

My heart has been a-twitter, my legs a-patter and my
mind a-flutter all day long (or dae lang, if Rabbi Burns –
Jewish, I wonder? – were to be believed) over the
problems posed by your last (hand-delivered!) letter,
which I found beside my teeth as I wiped the sleep from
my eyes last week. It is no simple problem, and neither of
us – both grown men, after all – should treat it as such,
per se. Among the questions raised by it are: a) Can one
choose foreign words? b) By 'favourite' are you judging
the sound of the word pure and simple or the marriage of
sound with meaning? c) If the answer to (b) is the latter,
then how would it be possible to choose a word for the
'least favourite' section which is both unpleasant in
sound but pleasant in meaning? For instance, the word
'*salami*' has a hideous, foreign, rather shifty ring to it, yet
of the meat itself I cannot have enough. d) Is one allowed
to choose a proper noun, or should we – as I think we
ought – create a new 'Proper Noun' section? If you are in
agreement with this last request, allow me to nominate
Zimbabwe, Cockfosters, Polystyrene, Scrofula and
Runcie as my five worst, and Toblerone, Badedas,
Primula, Bostik and Negus as my favourites. In the
'General' section, I would choose as my favourite all-
round words 'impish', 'chuckle', 'tiddly', 'tinkle' and
'smegma', and as my most grizzly, 'crèche', 'flush',
'suede', 'pontiff' and 'suite'.

To your other problem, I would have to answer 'yes',
for I can find no fault at all with Tony P.'s spelling – lucky,

for I don't believe that *A Dance to the Music of Tim* would have commanded such a dedicated league of readers.

No doubt this letter will find its way to you via the masterful menials at The Garrick (why do I always yearn to call it The Garlic?). I do hope you have not persuaded Hyacinth to venture abroad, as the European attitude to life (incidentally, what is Life?) is by no means her own: she tends to complain if she espies a foreigner in a railway carriage in England, so you can imagine how she reacted when I took her on a three week rail tour of Southern Italy for our honeymoon. All this brings me in a roundabout way to one of the topics raised by your letter *viz.* should you have interrupted our joint musings on the mysteries of the world for the sole purpose of tipping me the wink that you had more than half an eye for my wife, the aforesaid Hyacinth? This is the forty-four thousand dollar question. To be quite frank, I have always been of the school which believes that what is male is male and what is female is female, that chat about books and current events is male and that anything more *intime* (the French again) is tittle-tattle and therefore female. The Chinese have a word for it – Yin-and-Yang, the gobbledegook equivalent of our own much more straightforward 'His and Hers', but then as a race the Chinks have always been endlessly incorrigible, bless 'em. How hopelessly unclear one can be at times! Suffice it to say that this storm in a teacup is no skin off my nose, and Hyacinth was due for an airing anyway. If Lord Clark were sitting around a table with us today (alive and kicking, of course) I have no doubt that he would point us towards that neglected minor masterpiece, The Bible, which kicks off with, 'In the beginning was the Word'. It could only have been a short sprint after the Word that the letters began tumbling into the celestial pillar-boxes (delightful thought!) and thus civilisation set sail. Adam and Eve, that tiresome twosome, were very much an afterthought, and for all their snogging and canoodling they never managed to beat the Word into first place in the eyes of the good Lord (and I refer not to Kenneth!). So let our nibs continue to dance merrily across our stationery, let our Muses once more revel in the magic of the written word, untrained, unstrained and unrestrained! Could you please ask Hyacinth where I should bury her goldfish?

I have been mulling over your selection for the bouquet of funny tomes you are to set before the General Public (why is it always *General* Public, I wonder? Surely Lieutenant or even Private would be the more appropriate ranking (!!)). You are not, I trust, turning a blind eye to the Swan of Avon, for his plays are packed to bursting with hilarious 'comic relief'. Puns and ribaldry abound for the general merriment of those who keep their Shakespearian phrasebooks handy. I am happy to say that he shares my love of the lavatory when it comes to japes (or should it be jakes? – You see, it's infectious!). Of which is the funniest Shakespeare play, who's to say? I would personally direct my digit to the goodly *Hamlet*, best known, perhaps, for its more solemn moments, such as the grave-diggers scene, but an absolute howler when it gets into its stride, *viz* the 'orrible Ophelia, having got a little steamed up over a sherry too many, prattling on about everything inc. the Elsinore kitchen sink in utterly nonsensical fashion, or the 'apless 'amlet's 'To Be or Not to Be' ramble, which becomes a perfect scream if one recites it as 'Toby or not Toby', substituting other Christian names for words as it gathers pace. Bliss! Of course, what friend Leavis tended to forget was that the Bard wrote these plays *to be performed*, and not for eggheads to swat up and argue over. Thus, so-called soliloquies were shoved in so as to give the lads backstage a chance to deck the place out for the next scene; the 'comic relief' was designed to keep everyone awake through the major scenes; and the major scenes were there so that people wouldn't feel short-changed by the somewhat scant sight of a single chap mouthing a soliloquy. Excuse me while I climb down now from my soapbox, but do give *Hamlet* a spin in committee – I can see Pete Parker doubled up even as I write.

Do let me know how you are getting on with H. I fondly imagine you both strolling hand-in-hand (incidentally, I can assure you from my own experience that H.'s warts are *not* contagious) over some famous landmark – The Bridge of Sighs, maybe, or Land's End, spouting words curious and contemplative to each other. Bye the bye, Venice would anagram to Vice Den if only it contained a D! Alas, Hyacinth has forgotten to take her roller-skates, but do pass on to her the news that since Mr Pickwick seems to have taken such a shine to them, I have strapped them to his little feet, and I can't describe how adorable he looks rolling over, getting up, rolling over, *ad nauseam* throughout the day!

The television people visited me today, with wagonloads of picture-making paraphernalia and young men in 'jeans'. I dutifully recounted your *Samson Agonistes* anecdote, which they adored, and then went on to say how well your acting experience at school had served you in your occasional future career as a public speaker. Their ears pricked up when I dropped your appointment as Honorary Member of the Paedophile

Society, no less, to demonstrate how far your speeches had taken you, and they made it clear that they were simply dying to ask you all about it when they interviewed you. I said that I was only too glad to have been of help.

My regards to Hyacinth, and do remind her that her Sony Walkman should be worn about the ears, and not over the knees.

Yours ever,
Gerald

9 August 1983   *The Imperial Hotel*
                                             Bognor Regis

My dear Gerald,

I can't tell you how intensely agreeable was the sight of your timeless, formless handwriting upon the envelope forwarded to me by the good burghers of the Garrick. Both Hyacinth and I are cock-a-hoop that you have taken to her absence with such spirit, and though H. tends to worry that you might be having rather more fun with Mr Pickwick than is good for him (she tells me his tail is still loose from the ragging you subjected him to last Boxing Day) she is as delighted as I that our correspondence will continue to flourish willy-nilly. (Incidentally, I once had the honour to be introduced to the Original William Nilly by the late (and she was apt to be late even when she was alive!!) Rebecca West. He made his name as a publisher's reader for, I think, Cape's. He rarely reported on any book he was sent, but, when he did, they immediately knew that they should publish, regardless of his opinion, since the very fact that he had managed to finish it meant that it was short enough to foist on Mr and Mrs Joe Browzer. Delightful!)

As you may detect from the letter-heading, we have seen fit to make of Bognor Regis a temporary love-nest. Hyacinth is crowing over the resort and insists that before we leave we should look in on her old school chum Raine Spencer, whom she has not seen for fifty years, but sadly we must depart for London, that city full of buildings and people, tomorrow, so we are unlikely to entertain that opportunity. What a dark horse you have been, my dear Gerald, *re* your (now my) beloved Hyacinth. There are so many facets of her personality that you have placed firmly under the burning bushel. Before I came to know her so well, I knew from your letters that she was a dab hand at Origami, anagrams and metal-detecting, but imagine my surprise on being awoken after our first night together by her uncannily accurate impersonation of Neddy Seagoon of Goon Show fame squeaking out 'Wakey Wakey! Wakey Wakey!' in that blissfully funny voice of his. My surprise soon gave way to the most energetic chuckle I could muster, and this has encouraged her to treat me to a rendition of the aforementioned refrain once every two or three hours. She is anxious to extend this gift of hers, and for this reason she has suggested I buy her a record by one Paul Daniels, who is, she insists, a comedian.

I regret to say that work, that 'unquiet robber who skips as he steals', continues to pursue me, even midst an holiday. I received a form through the post today from the *Who's Who* organisation. Now, I suspect that you, my dear Gerald, have seldom if ever found cause to be pestered by the *Who's Who* bully-boys, for which I trust you are duly grateful, but once a human being, like myself, unwittingly reaches the higher echelons of the World of Letters, he is duty bound to submit an inventory of his achievements for the voracious consumption of a general public ever-hungry for details about the renowned. Up until today I have skilfully avoided any contact with *Who's Who* but now they have nailed me it would be churlish to avoid their approaches, so I have already filled in most of their wretched form – Parents, Education, Children, Club and so forth. But on coming to the section marked 'Recreations' I must admit to being a trifle stumped. I went through a phase of stamp collecting aged thirteen or so but soon disbanded my collection when the house doffer, a boy called Shaks (later to become Lord Chief Justice of Hendon), drew moustaches on all my Queen Victorias. Since then recreation *per se* has been *in absentia* from the life and times of Yours t. I read, of course, but 'Reading' coming from a publisher is unlikely to be believed. My girth testifies to my indifference to sport and I am supremely unmoved by the flickering images on the gogglebox (speaking of which, did you happen to apprehend 'Cor Blimey, Milord!' on the independent channel yesterday afternoon? As always, a sterling performance from that perennial jester, Ned Sherrin). So I am thinking of plumping for 'agreeably civilised company' or perhaps 'companionably agreeable civilisation', but I wish to supplement it with something a little lighthearted, so that I won't be taken for a cut-and-dried dyed-in-the-wool stick-in-the-mud. I was toying with 'twiddling my thumbs' (!!!) or 'cocking a snook at the philistines', though I am much taken with Cyril Smith's 'speaking my mind', Frederic Raphael's 'looking at myself in the mirror' (*pure* Freddie!) and Lord Delfont's deliciously witty 'supplying deprived youngsters with television sets'.

Since you now have time on your hands, and I am up to my n. in work (not forgetting your goodly (ex!) wife, who is, as I'm sure you remember, an absolute poppet, if a little demanding) I was wondering whether you could put your mind to cobbling together some sort of suitable recreation for me. I thought it might amuse you as you sit fretting during the wee wee hours (or wee-wee hours as Denis Norden once cheekily termed them!).

I have recently been alerted to the reason behind Melvyn Bragg's reluctance to engage me as his official biographer, *a priori, quid pro quo*. It emerges that he is tackling the job himself, under the provisional title *Me, Melvyn*.

Now that the Mother Teresa book has gone, as it were, 'up the spout' I am trying to get another one about her on the rails, under the working title *Nun Too Good*. Early days yet, but I have kicked off by sending word to Andrew Boyle – hush, hush, it goes without saying – that I would be prepared to offer ample remuneration if he were to come across proof positive that 'Mother' Teresa was up at Cambridge at the same time as friends Burgess, Philby and Maclean. Interesting, eh?

House-hunting will commence in earnest on our return to London. Clapham used to be regarded as the Back of Beyond, but is now considered pretty central, and I am reliably informed that Michael Horowitz arranges regular poetry-reading sessions on the Common, so we shall be commencing our searches there. It will also place me within spitting distance of Tubby W., whose letters are very nearly sewn up and in the bag. He was tickled pink by the Henry Kissinger correspondence, so I am in good odour, but he is now clamouring for the nigh impossible. He wishes there to be a series of letters intimating that he indulged in a clandestine *affaire d'amour* in the late Sixties with Jackie Kennedy. Well! As tall orders go, this one takes the biscuit. I told him firmly that it was John F. and not Jackie who was as randy as a rattlesnake, to use Keats' immortal phrase, but he swiftly quashed my objection by insisting that it was out of the question that he should be remembered by future generations for having had it away with a dead President. *Cui bono,* I happened to mention my dilemma to my new-found friend Henry Kissinger – he of the prawn-cocktail-and-chips in Tavistock – and, quick as a flash, he called his relish-tray girl to the phone. Her name (*too* extraordinary, I agree) is Jill Kennedy and she readily agreed to dash off the odd *billet doux* to Tubby in the style of her more illustrious namesake in return for three Julio Inglesias records. I am still awaiting her first effort but will keep you *eau fey* with the situation as it develops.

The next meeting of the Funny Books committee is scheduled for the day after tomorrow, and I look forward to availing myself of the opportunity to gen up on Prince H. of D. whilst tottling back to the metrop. on the train. Far gone now are the days when the steam of the locomotive, billowing out of the shuttlecocks like leaves from a book, would deposit a rich, furry envelope of glory over one's pickle sandwiches, when the 'ppoowweepp! ppoowweepp!' of the steam whistle would summon children from far and wide to the tracks, their shrieks and squeals rising to a crescendo of juvenile reverie as the big wheels thundered o'er them. Yet the memory remains, and was it not that wise old bird Dr Johnson who first observed that 'He who is without memory is destined to forget'? Nowadays, the 'modern' trains with their push-button ventilation, their easy-swivel seats and their double-glazed spitoons may well have stream-lined the pressures on the businessman, but surely we have lost something indivisible and immovable? Such is Progress – 'that silver-tinted tongue of ill-ease' as Noele Gordon once called it. But I ramble.

My dear Gerald, Hyacinth is insistent that you redirect any envelope from Sotheby's to her c/o this

humble scribbler at The Garrick post haste. It will
contain the 'lovely lolly' vouchsafed us from H.'s forays
into the world of metal-detecting.

Happy days!

Yours ever,
Harvey

114

My dear Harvey,

Though the heading atop this vellum reads
'Bookends' it might just as well read 'Pure Bliss' or
'Seventh Heaven', for I am lolling in the very lap of
luxury, gleefully gallivanting in the glades of gloating
gladness, thumbing through the thickets of thankfulness,
skipping saucily o'er shiploads of socks: in a nutshell
(why, I wonder, is it *always* a nutshell? The blessed things
are so damnably irritating that I can't see anyone in his
right mind wishing to place *anything* in them, quite apart
from the inevitable ensuing struggle to get anything *out*
of them (!)) I have discovered the meaning of Liberty
Yes, I have *found myself*; none of your spiritual search
parties for me – I have found myself nestling 'twixt the
arm of that uncomfortable old armchair of which
Hyacinth was so inordinately fond (temporarily
converted I might add into an hotel of some luxury for
my new pet mice) and the gramophone, perched upon
H.'s collection of old Burl Ives records, my superglue in
one hand, my pen in the other, and in the other – no, I
jest, I am still limited to one pair of hands, tho' I feel as if
I have six or seven (sweet dream – just think of the tomes
all those mitts could produce, and how many more they
could handle; was it not Winston (bless him) who first
pointed out to a disbelieving gen. pub. that half a dozen
men could manage six times the amount of work of one
man?) and I am quite beside myself that there is no
longer anyone beside me (the old puns again!) and I must
regretfully (Ho, Ho, pull the other, Hardy (Nelson, of

course)) announce the refurbishment (awful Spanish word) of *la maison* in oodles of varying modes, some classical, some romantic, some *fin de siècle*, some *sui generis*, some *fête champêtre* and others *infra dig*, some *à la mode* and others *à la carte*, some *billet doux* and still others *non sequitur* - an agreeable mish-mash, then, of the sort of *sotto-voce fait accompli* that sits well in a bachelor abode, but let me detail the changes for the edification of H. and your good self: first (*never* firstly, though occasionally thirsty (!!)) I have imported a veritable army of white mice (luckily on the very same day that Mr Pickwick came a cropper in the spin-dryer!) and I have already named them after each of The Nolan Sisters – there goes Cheryl up my left trouser leg even as I write! – so I now feel I always have someone to squeak to (forgive the awful pun!) and, unlike the Human Race, no names, no pack drill, nothing could be further from their dear little minds than a three-hour game of Scrabble; second, I have got into the habit of taking all my meals from the basin in the downstairs cloakroom – pure joy, since it spells the end of washing-up, odious business, and the gentle tilt of the sides ensures that for my beloved baked bean casseroles only a spoon is necessary; third, I have removed all Hyacinth's pictures from the walls, including, I might add, her own stabs at 'Notre Dame Come Rain or Shine' spraypainted in acrylic, and I have substituted them with my long-treasured, seldom-exhibited posters of Fatty 'Codger' Barnacle in his celebrated 1909 comedy performance as Lord 'Fingers' Goodman (incidentally, did you happen to catch Alan Coren's marvellous skit in which he intentionally mistook Goodman for a Good Man? – Hilarious!) and fourthly (allowable) I have buttonholed a small but thriving section of our Great British Workforce ('Pull the other', as Tom Driberg used to bellow!) to pour what I believe is known as concrete over Hyacinth's garden, so as to provide a clear landing space for my little mouse friends, who have recently taken to skydiving – I fix them up with large handkerchieves harnessed to their little bodies with household string and then they demand that I throw them from an upstairs window (wasn't it Emile Zola, or at very least one of his detectives, who first noted that anything worth doing can be done from an upstairs window?) whereupon they swoop to *terra firma*, their little legs wiggling for all they're worth (which, let's face it, isn't much!) and so these are the household changes per *pro tem*, though I daresay I might get fidgety this afternoon and move the bath into the sitting room (I jest, of course – it is already there!!), but enough of 'Bookends' and let us move on to our more customary *sujets*, for inst. your prob. *re* a suitable 'Recreation' for *Who's What*, over which I, who, as an humble retired schoolmaster, have never been approached by that august publication, have been racking my b.'s, upcoming with one or two suggestions for a lighthearted entry, such as 'widdling over Bloomsbury first editions', 'sucking up to power or money (in no particular order)' or 'rooting out the second rate (and publishing it)' – I would have thought that any or all of these would send a smirk across the visage of even the most dour W's W reader, and the whole world loves a chap who can crack a joke agin' himself, as the immeasurable Roy Hattersley discovered long ago, bless him and his grasp of the essential paradoxes of modern life – for instance, only this merry morn (or 'merry mourn' as the Indictable Max used to call the funerals of his nearest and d'st!) I was contemplating the paradox of the envelope from Sotheby's addressed to Hyacinth and yet – *and herein lies the irony* – opened by Mr Mouse himself, *ie*, me, and the paradox does not stop at that juncture, my dear Harvey, no, it continues like the babbling brook o'er the crock of gold, for what should be in that envelope, what should be contained in that thin brown papyrus, folded over onto itself and stuck up (aren't we all?!) with a gluey substance, bearing the legend 'Sothebys and Co Ltd'? A hefty cheque for forty-four thousand of Coutts' crispest and cleanest smackers? Why, no! Paradoxically, the aforementioned envelope contains nothing of the sort, but rather a most charming message signed 'p.p. Graham Postlethwaite' (how often, don't you find, representatives of companies have those very same initials – but let us not get sidetracked on that hinterland of conceptual mathematics – *ie* the coincidence) stating that alas and alack H.'s solid gold 'find' is in fact the property of the Birmingham City Corporation, from whom it disappeared without trace in 1965, and is consequently unauctionable (awful word). Knowing how you relish the unexpected, I'm sure your face on reading this info. will be a veritable sight to see, made all the more joyous by the yelps of H., who really comes into her own (her own what, I wonder?) on receiving a startle of this sort. I enclose Mr Postlethwaite's pleasing missive, and also a brief but kindly note from a Councillor Hatchett of the Birmingham City Corporation Museums Department thanking H. for her diligent work in the metal-detecting situation and trusting that she will accept with the Corporation's compliments a free day-pass to the full range of Birmingham's galleries, exhibitions and museums (excluding the Museum of Wickerwork, closed for renovation until December, 1986) – quite a feather in H.'s cap, I'm sure you will agree, and worthy of pride of place in the bedroom of your new flat (I am told Tooting is becoming immensely fashionable).

Do offer H. my fondest congratulations.

Yours ever,
Gerald.

P.S. What is your favourite method of walking? I myself place one foot in front of the other (which necessarily involves the leg, or legs) and, repeating this process *quid pro quo* find myself ambulating with some efficiency. And you?

P.P.S. I enclose a passage from Bernard Levin's delicious book *Enthusiasms* – no small influence on my own style, I think you'll agree!!

'Of the many pleasures our rich and lusty world has to offer, and I think now of the sublime majesty of Poussin's "Dejeuner Sur l'Herbe", the infinitely glorious jottings of one such as Katherine Ferrier ("one such as" indeed! there could be no other), the unforced intricacy of a Beethoven, the lesser, but no less valuable, pleasure of a boiled egg topped with the merest smattering of *le ketchupe tomate*, the unsealed heights of a Larkin haiku, the blazing subtlety of the ninth paragraph of Forster's Raj Quartet, the intrepid cavortings of Picasso as he welds his paintbrush so firmly and yet so delicately to the canvas, the uplifting and curiously elegaic feeling of elation one experiences in the interval of a

Wagner operetta, the unforeseen glories of the down-to-earth and, on occasion, ribald good sense of Messrs Morecambe and Wise, the lesser, but never to be undervalued, pleasure of conversing with friends on a south-facing *balconie* of the excellent Taj Mahal hotel in Hong Kong, that city of cities ("for there is no city wherein there is no building" – Marlowe) as the sun disappears slowly over the horizon, casting its gentle beams to and fro o'er the ripples of the fast-ebbing sea, like a thought of Goethe, the exquisite, but no less minor, pleasure of consuming three dozen oysters *au Rhum Baba*, before embarking upon breakfast, the contemplative passion of a Montaigne minuet – why, the list is, as Falstaff said to young Huck, approaching a panundrum of possibilities – the pleasure for to which I would go with Lady Macbeth to the ends of the earth therein to participate in the inestimable joy – there can be no other word – of what is known in German as *Meingottachtungspitfeuer* and along the noble shores of England, oh, all right then, Britain, as breaking wind: that outrush of malodorous, to some, but never to oneself, into the vast mysteries of the earth's atmosphere, having first circulated amongst the very heart and lungs of man, so that, in some bizarre and yet readily explicable way, the air that will in, will out: an enactment, surely, of what Kahlil Karmen hints at in his *Wanderings Through Simla in a Daimla* when he says, in his customarily gentle and persuasive tones, on the subject, if I remember rightly, correct me dear reader if my memory, never faultless, has, in one of those turns of fate so beloved by the Furies, slipped not just up but sideways, downwards and headlong: we are none of us, not even Messrs Scargill and Benn and their merry cohorts, perfect, of divine grace (I refer not to that exhortation to the Almighty or Almighties before bread is broken in all the most proper households, including, I might add, my own): "Let man's heart be full, for tomorrow we dine" and, this being demonstrated with every fresh wind that is broken, we find that, by a process approaching osmosis, by both taking in and later expelling hot air, we are hourly reminded of our mortality, our short voyage 'twixt birth and death aboard this mortal coil': so too are our minds jogged to recapture wind already broken, wind broken whilst savouring the delicate intensity of a Vermeer landscape (I swear you can actually *scape* that land!), whilst striding, hat sitting prettily on head, down Ogden Nash's Regent Street, whilst rustling one's programme in anticipation of hearing Mantovani's 5th in D minor, whilst discussing with close friends the relationship – for such it was – between Wagner and his late wife Natalie, whilst observing the moon throwing up its luminous rays over the Ponte Vecchio, whilst sipping Arriviste Excellente Five Star Brandy to the lilt of a ballad by Mr Thomas Jones, yes, by hook or by crook, and, on occasion, by both, I would, and that is not too strong a word, trample o'er water and swim through straw to catch within the sensitive framework of my own nostril ("Oh what a piece of work is man!"), be it my left nostril or my right nostril is a matter of small import, the slightest whiff of my own air, long ago ejected, ne'er forgotten, and now, within the discipline of its own effusion, like Tamburlaine's rooks, come back to rest. At any rate, that's what I think.'

6 September 1983   *The Hotel Exelsior*
                                              London E. 18

My dear Gerald,

Many, many thanks for your highly felicitous and life-enhancing letter, and for forwarding, and saving us the bother of opening, the generous letter from Councillor Hatchett of the Birmingham City Corporation Museums Department and the admittedly somewhat disappointing letter from Mr. Postlethwaite of Sotheby's.

How very fascinating you were on the subjects of paradox and coincidence, and how very right you are when you ajudge my lifelong interest in these interwoven chains. Whether it falls in the territory of paradox or coincidence, I know not, but on the very same day your intensely agreeable letter arrived, Hyacinth mistook your voluminous manuscript for a load of old rubbish and hurled it with some force into the dustbin. Alas it was only as we were watching the Refuse Disposal Officers (I refer of course to the common or garden Dustmen!) pouring the contents of our bin into the vast shredder at the back of their cart ('Mobile Refuse Disintegrator', no doubt!) that we realised that your *Pass the Fruitcake, Iris* had gone for the proverbial Burton, lock, stock and b. Hyacinth assures me that you kept no copy of the late masterpiece, which makes its total and utter destruction all the more poignant. I would suggest that you seek solace not only in the paradoxical delight of twelve years' work being reduced to nothing in the course of five minutes, but also in the words of Oscar: 'If a thing is worth doing, it is worth not doing at all'. Delightful! Of course, talking now on a strictly professional basis, if you should have any idea for yet another book, I would be only too happy to consider it.

I too walk employing the method described in the charming postscript to your tidings. You don't mention whether you avail yourself of the use of a pair of shoes, placed on the feet to prevent unnecessary soreness, though, if my memory serves, I rather think that you do. I find them indispensable, particularly if one is walking over any surface which generally doesn't 'get on well' with the bare undersole – glass, for instance, can be extremely treacherous, and any ground providing refuge for thorns, tin tacks or sharp stones is potentially most hazardous for the barefooted. Have you ever tried 'running'? It involves placing one foot in front of the other in quick succession, so that the effect is very much like walking at speed. It is becoming increasingly popular on the dreaded gogglebox, particularly in American 'detective' series, wherein the villain, having left his motor-car in an heap, is obliged to flee at a pace swifter than even the healthiest walk. Not for us, I agree, but as we are both avid collectors of Gen. Kno., I thought I might just drop it in.

I greatly enjoyed your priceless suggestions for my 'recreation', though on reflection I have decided to plump for the more formal 'overseeing those societies and associations of which I am an Honoured Member, nurturing their qualities, diminishing their defects, acclimatising them to a fuller appreciation of their societal roles and helping to more fully integrate them in the infrastructure of our times'. Earlier in the form, I mention my position in both the Worshipful Company of Authors and in The Paedophile Association, thus giving those worthy organisations a welcome boost, and it seemed churlish to destroy this bit of much-needed advertising for them with a flip comment later on.

The Humorous Books committee continues to gather steam. Harold Wilson's *The Governance of Britain* is now among the definites, as is Tony Benn's immortal memoir of political life in the '70s, *Let's Not Drag Personalities Into It. Diary of a Nobody* is there, of course (who could forget that scene wherein dear, poor old Pooter admonishes young Denzil for losing the can opener, thus forcing Captain Grimes to employ a tin of pineapples during the legendary cricket match?), and we felt duty bound to include at least one volume of Craig Raine's deliciously witty poems, so after much discussion we went straight for *The Onion, Memory,* mainly I admit because of that rib-tickling comma. We still have many, many places to fill (I am pushing Freddie Raphael's wicked spoof on literary criticism, *Cracks from the Lice* for all I'm worth) so if your much-pilfered brain can dig anything else up, Tim, Pete and I would be needlessly grateful.

And so to my (your?) dear Hyacinth, who, moneyed or not, will always be Hyacinth, warts and all. Three days before your letter arrived, when we were still counting our proverbial feathered friends, I agreed to delay our departure to the capital in order that H. might call in on her old school chum, Raine Spencer. Raine is, as you must surely know by now, the President of The Old Unspeakables, a charity organisation that seeks to provide a warm hearth and good cheer to foreign businessmen of all ages, creeds and nationalities. Though I have never met Raine personally, I am said to be favoured for the post of Literary Advisor to the said organisation and as the renowned Bishop Gleaves once remarked, 'There is nothing so handy as the Personal Touch', so I felt it would be in my own interest to trot along for the ride, as it were.

Bognor Regis, nestling 'neath the warm left elbow of the Sussex Downs, noisy yet quiet, colourful yet uniform, old yet new, bristling with the candid openness of the holiday resort, and yet curiously private, is a relatively small town, stubborn, cowardly, grateful, scornful, God-fearing, atheistical, and one would be hard-pressed to find an inhabitant who could not direct you without so much as a moment's thought to the seat of Earl Spencer. As Jonathan Raban noted in his brilliantly imaginative travelogue, *In the Steps of Paul Theroux*, 'the English are an Island Race, for whom the sea, swaying and bustling like an ocean of corn, is essentially different from the land', and probably for this reason most of the major houses in Bognor Regis are constructed, most wisely in my opinion, on dry land. Be that as it may, Hyacinth and I picked our way with some ease through the streets of this town, which remains to this day beside the sea, and soon found ourselves outside the discreet portals of the elegant 'Spencer Grange', recognisable only from the life-size statues of The Prince and Princess of Wales situated towards the middle of the front lawn and the souvenir kiosk to the left of the shiny gold front gates. After some small debate amongst ourselves as to the *modus vivendi* of attaining access to the interior, we soon hit upon the idea of seeking help from the jocular lady in the plastic tiara who was, at that moment, manning the kiosk. Blow me down, but who should it be but Raine, Countess Spencer, Baroness of Ongar, Upholder of The Silver Export, Mistress of the Fleece and President of the Old Unspeakables.

'Cigarettes, souvenirs, confectionery, ices, can I help you?' said Raine with the well-rounded manner of the true aristocrat. 'Remember me?' exclaimed Hyacinth. There was a small silence. 'I'm not sure I er – ' said Raine, tactfully. 'Not a lot, not a lot' chirped Hyacinth. She was to explain to me in the railway carriage afterwards that this was the well-known catchphrase of the comedian, Mr Paul Daniels. It obviously struck a chord in Raine, who quick as a flash proffered a twin-pack of Wrigley's Spearmint Chewing Gum, suggesting we accept them 'on the house'. As well as being a gesture of consummate graciousness, it gave her small opportunity to dredge the mud-slicks of her mind for any dim recollection of Hyacinth. Eventually, a glimmer of recognition appeared to flicker o'er her brow. 'Could it have been Blackpool, the year before last, when Johnnie and myself flicked the switch on the world-famous illuminations?' she ventured, then, perhaps noting the odd look in H.'s eyes, she added, 'Of course, you would have been on the Municipal Committee, no mistake.'

I need hardly mention that Hyacinth looked as put out as the proverbial cat. But she soon perked up. 'If I mentioned "Stain her bath, Romulus; shag the rules!" would that find you any warmer?' Hyacinth repeated. 'I'm sorry' said Raine, a note of irritation creeping into her inflection, 'You've lost me.'

'I'll give you a clue, then' said Hyacinth. 'Think in anagram terms.'

'If you'll excuse me, I must rearrange the Princess Di facecream display' said Raine, bustling beneath the counter.

'Saint Bartholomew's School for Girls!' said Hyacinth. Eliciting no response, she continued, 'It's the anagram of "Stain her bath, Romulus; shag the rules!" Roughly.'

'I'm sorry. I'm still not with you and I'm very busy. I haven't the foggiest what you're on about,' snapped Raine. It soon emerged that Raine was most definitely *not* the Raine Spencer with whom H. had been to school and felt little or no desire to make amends for that sorry social *hiatus*. I attempted to soften the busy Countess by shelling out twenty-five new pence for a postcard of her and her husband modelling a new and inexpensive line of swimwear on the beach at Brighton. I considered it temperate not to mention my candidature for the post of Literary Advisor to her charity, and bundled Hyacinth away as speedily as a fireman's lift would allow.

A vale of tetchiness hung over our return journey. To most of my questions Hyacinth would simply sigh or start humming tunes from the 'Best of George Formby' and whenever I attempted to broaden the non-existent discussion with references to the World of Literature – what did she think of John Cowper Powys's little known *œuvre*, *The Nature of the Meaning behind the Soul of Mankind* for instance, or how did she square Professor Calculus's remote humanity with Nestor's generous inhumanity, her only reply would be 'Not a lot, not a lot'. With the arrival of the news from Sotheby's, I sensed that an essential part of our relationship (awful word) had somehow disappeared. But, my dear Gerald, why should your ears be bothered with petty problems? Was it not Saint Augustine (You'd have to be a saint with a name like that!!) who said that the essence of all Evil is too little cash up front? Equally, one could apply that stricture to all problems common to humanity from the bowler-hatted lesbian brigade to the Scottish fisherman rounding up his herd. If only Peter Jay, with his *Mission to Explain* were still alive.

Hyacinth continues to speak highly of you. (Paradoxically, she speaks higher of you than of me. Female!)

Have you ever read a book *all the way through?* I'm told it's well worth the effort.

Yours ever,
Harvey

18 September 1983   *Bookends*

My dear Harvey,

Your last letter was a veritable cornucopia of palatability. To respond to your last point first (!) – yes, I have indeed read a number of works all the way through, though not, admittedly, for more years than I care to remember. I once read Gibbon's *Decline and Fall of the Roman Empire* all the way through, but once I had finished the title I couldn't find the energy to wade through the book as well. Dear Oscar (bless him!) noted that 'If fewer people read books, less books would be read' and he strongly supported the Latinate tradition of seeing a book essentially as a *tool*, a view to which his own house bore testament: here *Marius the Epicurean* propping up a card table, there a first edition De Quincey acting as a primitive ping-pong bat, and over there in the corner, the poor benighted Mrs Wilde squashing a fly with *Lyrical Ballads*. I have recently evolved a method of reading the Classics which saves oodles of time and injects a much needed *frisson* of humour into the gloom-merchants. One reads only those pages whose numbers go odd–even–odd (e.g. 325). This does away with the first one hundred 'getting to know you' pages and reduces the others to the jolliest of japes. For a long while I have been meaning to re-read Tony Powell's immortal masterpiece, *An Dance to the Music of Time* (still read today, I wonder?), but I have been unable to fit it into my punishing schedule of training the mice (they now enact scenes from 'The Bridge over the River Kwai', with me as the Commanding Officer of the Japs and them as the prisoners – escapees, I need hardly tell you, are firmly stamped upon!) and rearranging the house (I have entirely done away with the bath *per se* – the space is ideal for an auxiliary mouse detention centre). Nevertheless, using my method I will be able to skip through the entire *oeuvre* in a matter of minutes, and if one finds out slightly less about the exotic but sinister journalist Scant Pebble, the ruthless but adorable M.P. Hardy Scrofula, the cheerful but depressed society hostess, Primula Cheese, and the deceitful but essentially honest publisher, Clandestine Hump, well, so much the better.

Your fears for the safety of my *Pass the Fruitcake, Iris*, are most touching, but, I am delighted to say, quite unfounded. I may have intimated in the past that the copy in your fair hands was *le sole bonne femme*, but happily I was fibbing. My goodly bank manager, Mr Cornhill, has been keeping a copy under lock and key, though, thus far, there have been few if any desperadoes with sawn-off shotguns attempting to knuckle their way into the safe, there to partake of a first reading of my manuscript. So breathe again, dear Harvey; your chance to publish a minor masterpiece is still intact. Perhaps this will cause your spirits to be lifted out of the doldrums (so named, the ineffable Partridge informs me, after Lord and Lady Doldrum, an unexciting 18th century couple from Kent, much given to entertaining guests with their reminiscences of the previous evening's Bridge – hence the phrase 'stuck in the Doldrums': Delicious!). You will be similarly uplifted, no doubt, by my addition of an agreeable appendix of certainly no more than fifty pages, in which, indulging in a little 'Poet's Licence', I have a lot of fun culling some of my own (previously unpublished and, indeed, unperformed) comedy sketches of the last thirty years, many of them written with celebrated performers 'in mind'. Here is a little snippet I wrote for that cheerful duo, Morecambe and Wise, just to get your taste-buds wagging their tails *à la Pavlov*.

Eric:	Hello, who's this coming along with the short fat hairy legs?
Ernie:	It's me, Ernie. And who may you be, oh fat one with the glasses?
Eric:	I'm Eric, of course.
Ernie:	I've written a new play.
Eric:	Good. Well, let's go and *play*. (*laughter*) What's it about, then?
Ernie:	It's about twenty pages long. (*laughter*) And it concerns the death of President Kennedy.
Eric:	Who's he when he's at home? (*laughter*)
Ernie:	The late President of the United States of America, that's who.
Eric:	We can't have someone who's *late*. He'll never make it in time for the show. (*laughter*)
Ernie:	You're right. It may not be *wise*.
Eric:	No – you're *wise* (*i.e. Ernie Wise*) he's Kennedy. (*laughter*)
Ernie:	Now I'm with you.
Eric:	Better than being without me, and that's for sure. (*laughter*)

And so the good-natured banter marches on, much to the general merriment of both audience and performers alike. I have not yet sent the script to the said jesters, anxious as I was that your company, my dear Harvey, should scoop all the *kudos*[1] first, but I have no doubt that the very second they see it 'on the page', as it were, they will do their utmost to squeeze it into one of their television 'specials'. They know better than anyone in the

[1] *Kudos, kuditos* (Greek): Literally, money.

business how very hard it is for *un ecriveur* to enter into the very soul of a performer and still come out with humorous remarks. So that you are not plunged once more into the embarrassing position of having to admit that you stood by as a masterpiece was shredded into a thousand and one little pieces, I will take it upon myself (why is it always *upon* oneself, never *underneath* oneself or even *in front* of oneself?) to deliver the manuscript – plus appendix – directly to the printers, thus by-passing the somewhat light fingers of your good self.

Your vignette of Hyacinth's meeting with Raine Spencer had me quite doubled up. You may or may not know that H.'s grove of Academe, St Bartholomew's, was more a remand centre than a fully fledged school for young ladies (it was there that she picked up her penchant for placing pilfered products in her pockets and then pitter-pattering away without paying, though this charming forgetfulness may become more evident as that fickle forty-four thousand starts making its goodbyes even more heartfelt!) so I must say I always considered it *most* unlikely that she had encountered the jewel in the crown of one of our foremost aristocratic families at such a frankly (whatever happened to frankness?) sordid place of learning. Incidentally is it not a symptom of *nos jours*, a veritable bunion on the backside of egalitarianism, that snobbery is now regarded with such unhealthy contempt, as if it were something to be swept under the Wilton and not to be gratefully acknowledged for what it always was – the guiding force behind the great tide towards self-improvement which has carried with it such unavoidable mortals as Disraeli and Kipling, and, in our own time, Margaret Thatcher (bless her!) and Paul Johnson, whose volume of Collected Essays, *It Gets Up*

My Nose reveals him as committed today as he has ever been, though some might argue that he has never been committed for long enough. Once again, you must excuse me while I lay my hobby-horse to one side and return, hands a-clapping, to the rest of the Nursery of Life, there to peruse the multifarious *maelstrom* of gifts that God has set before us, some with batteries not provided, some in need of a little stuffing, some perhaps a little scratched and jaded, but all of them there to be flung around and enjoyed. But I ramble.

As you might divine (divine!) from my tone, my mood of optimism continues unabated. An *éminence grease* such as yourself, while basking in the coveted limelight of city grandeur (and *chacun à son goo*, as Clemmie Freud quipped in one of his priceless articles on food) can become too easily entangled in what Oscar once termed 'the sullen profundity of trivia' whilst the likes of me find that unlauded, unapplauded and never knowingly undersold as the countryside might be, it allows its inhabitants an ease by which they may contemplate the great issues of the Universe, and still come out smiling. Was it not Tom Eliot, old Stearns himself, who characterised the great issues as Birth, Copulation and Death? Pardon me if I appear frivolous, but how can sex be more important than one hundred and one other things, for instance, drawing randomly from my top hat, a nice house, pleasant food, congenial company, a well-stocked wine cellar, a good book and perhaps an after-dinner mint or two? Heaven knows whether you have attempted the aforementioned activity with H. or nay, but if you have indeed taken the plunge I am sure you will consider my after-dinner mint comparison a little far-fetched, a solitary Toffo or an half-chewed marshmallow being a little more appropriate. One could argue the toss with T.S.E. over Birth and Death until the cows came home (though he was not, to my knowledge, a betting man) but for the life of me I cannot see how it makes any difference whether or nay one *thinks* about the blessed things 'til one's blue in the face. As you will no doubt recall from your days as a Classics scholar, my dear Harvey, the word 'intellectual' has its stem in the Latin 'lectus' meaning, literally, 'a fop, a braggart, a whiner', and though one can think of intellectuals who don't play on that pitch (Clive James's sense is entirely common, for instance) the vast maj. shilly-shally around fretting over what Leavis characterised as 'The Great Unmentionables', leaving the rest of mankind to worry about the Business of Living.

But as the rosy hue of summer (did you by any chance catch Alan Coren's enchanting skit wherein he (intentionally) mistook 'Rosy Hugh' for a somewhat sloshed transvestite? Delicious!) makes way for the iridescent glow of autumn, we country folk find little time to partake either in the party intrigues of London's High Society or in the pettifogging intellectual niceties of the High Tables of Oxbridge. Instead we busy ourselves with the more down-to-earth pursuits, so well described by Laurie Lee in his autobiography of the last ten years, *Cider, Five Pints of Best, a Couple of Guinnesses, Five Large Whiskies and a Brandy Chaser with Rosie:* 'Gently as onions our hands, gnarled but murmuring, gripped the logs, wooden as the Ark, cautious in their asphalt silence; mischievous as the daffodil, the water would bubble and twist, scorched by the flames our own knuckles had wrought: therein lay our contentment, as plangent and handsome as the prayer of a mule bearer.'

My telephone has been abuzz with marvellously excited television producers asking me all about your activities as a young man, your friendship with Tom Driberg, your membership of the Paedophile Society and your *fête champêtre* with Hyacinth. Luckily for them (not only the independent company now, but also Lord Reith's estimable British Broadcasting Corporation and a variety of news organisations, both national and international) they found me in one of my most chatty of moods, and they later said that I could not have been more helpful. You cannot imagine how delightful it is to me that an ex-pupil of mine is creating such a stir.

Yours ever,
Gerald

My dear Gerald,

How very tedious the Mass Media can be to those of
us who have taken it upon ourselves to edge this barbaric
world we live in just that bit closer to a state which could
reasonably be called Civilisation, and, worse, they badger
our friends as well. But from the tone of your comments,
it appears that you have taken all those darned telephone
calls in your stride, and I trust that this is so. I must say it
is most gratifying to be at last given the sort of exposure
that has, and I say this with all modesty, long been my
due. Too often the true fire-bearers of a nation's culture
perish with their flags unfurled, their praises unsung,
their phrases unhung, so it will come as a shot in the arm
to all those whose words remain unread that an ordinary
mortal such as myself, who has dedicated himself to the
world of letters, should now achieve the recognition of
his peers in an hurly-burly of television exposure. My
interviews are not scheduled for some two weeks: they
tell me they are waiting for some government report or
other, presumably on the future of publishing or the
nurturing of talent.

I simply could not contain my chortles at your
delicious Morecambe and Wise sketch; so much so,
indeed, that I must insist that work of this quite
exceptional quality should not be premiered to the man
on the Clapham Omnibus (these days, I'll lay you evens
he's a fare-dodger!) by means of the (let's face it)
somewhat fuddy-duddy medium of the bundle of refined
wood we commonly call the Book; rather, it should come

to him from the lips of the entertainers for whom it was written. Morecambe and Wise would lap up a sketch of that hilarity, so let's hear no more of this appendix nonsense: send it to 'em right away!

Once again, Mr Coincidence places his estimable digit on the doorbell of life. My ears turned the colour of redcurrant jelly (how rarely one is offered the real thing these days – is nothing immune to supermarketisation?) upon seeing Pres. Kennedy crop up in your uproarious 'sketch'. Extraordinary! As I write, I am conducting a detailed reading of a manuscript for which only the word 'amazing' (in actual fact a perfectly decent word often employed by the early Christian fathers, as Philip Howard has pointed out in his first-class *New Words for Old Rope*) will suffice. Under the provisional title of The Phenomenon Phile and penned over a period of twenty years by Dr Kurt V. Janov, it lays powerful claim to be the single most important book since early von Daniken. With extensive reference to photographs, many of them in focus, and with much to-ing and fro-ing with the lighter side of ballistics, Janov provides convincing evidence that it was not President Kennedy who was murdered in Dallas on 22nd November 1963, but rather his wife, Jackie. Though no summary, however brief, can do justice to Janov's powerful, 900 page thesis, it appears that there was a blackout in the couple's aeroplane changing room as they were heading for Dallas, the upshot of which was that they found themselves stepping out into the hot Dallas sunshine, waving to the rapturous crowds, decked out in each other's garb. The assassin or assassins, whether employed by the KGB or C&A, then took their potshots at the wrong person, causing considerable embarrassment to the powers that be, who immediately instigated our old friend, the cover-up. At last it all becomes clear: the secrecy surrounding the corpse, the discrepancies in official accounts, the murder of Lee Harvey Oswald, who had obviously realised his mistake. Life after the assassination cannot have been easy for John F. Kennedy, and once all this is out, I feel certain the American public will feel more sympathetic to the break-up of his marriage to Aristotle Onassis. What say you? Pretty stirring stuff, eh? Needless to say, best kept under your sou'wester for the time being.

Where *did* you locate that delicious spoonful of pure Oscar? His gift for juggling with the very meaning of words, turning them on their heads, shaking them by the ankle and giving them a sharp smack on their behinds is second to none. 'The sullen profundity of trivia' – it quite literally sparkles on the page, as iridiscent as a maypole, as succulent as a spring lamb yelping merrily amongst the hedgerows, as true as you or I (you or me? one could argue the toss 'til the cows redomiciled themselves – oh, the puzzles set us by our endlessly riddlesome – but interminably fascinating – language!). How often the pestilential modern world forgets that words are what Sir Laurence Lamb once succinctly described as 'wisdom's flagship' – that is to say that they are not *of themselves* of interest unless they are conveying some nugget of pith to the erstwhile reader. This is still comprehended in The East (or 'The Yeast' as the Inedible Max was wont to term it!!!) and for this reason I have been turning more and more to those distant lands for my spiritual nourishment, and I must say they do fill one's platter to o'erflowing. Your Bernard Levin (estimable mind, and funny with it) was pure bliss: it was in fact he who first thrust *Sea and Sun – The Thoughts of Kahlil Karmen* into my pocket over dinner at The Garrick (shallotts braised in emulsifier followed by tender noisette d'agneau in a lambswool sauce, with sponge coddled in armagnac to follow, washed down with a particularly fine Dutch mountain champagne) and I have been savouring it ever since. 'As the song thrush makes his home in the deepest river, as the cloud ploughs the land of his fathers, as the distant sailor lays his head on the willow bush, so does the banished warrior yearn for the enslaved worm.' How intensely rich and positively life-enhancing such a sentence can be, meaning something different to all who read it. Karmen's more aphoristic utterances are well worthy of note too – 'The empty bottle holds no liquid'; 'The fish cannot swim with a sock over his head'; 'No building remains standing that is made of bricks'; 'The man with no pockets must place his shoes on his feet'; and so on. They have all, I admit most readily, helped me through these difficult, nay, trying, times.

Difficult? I hear you ask. Trying? But is not my dear Harvey enjoying quasi-connubial bliss with my ex? Alas, my dear Gerald, how wrong, how very wrong you are. I have never been a man for whom a conscience is a mere 'kerchief, to be removed from some inner pocket when – and only when – the nose starts playing up. No, my conscience is very much more akin to the nose itself – permanently and forever there, come rain or shine. And at the present moment, my dear Gerald, it is dripping. I beg you, Gerald, as my oldest friend, to be, as it were, my handkerchief, and let me breathe easy once more.

Let me be plain ('But you are, madam, but you are' –

Winston to B. Braddock – delicious!). I have long felt
that the complexion of our friendship was to some extent
– no matter how small – altered when your Hyacinth
chose to throw in her lot with myself: on my side, there
was intense guilt (did you by any chance catch Miles
Kington's beautifully crafted piece in which he
(intentionally) confused guilt with gilt? Splendid stuff)
and I sensed that on your side, behind the elation of the
solitary (Hermione Lee's poignant phrase) there lay a
chap playing on a sticky wicket, only too desperate to
regain that which was rightfully his, viz. his dear wife. It
has been said that only poets and gods know the true
meaning of love. Though I am myself a member of
neither of those not inconsiderable breeds, I am a
publisher, and, as such, I have seen many varieties of
men, and, on occasion, women, and I have experienced
much of the vast spectrum of emotions on offer to the
sensitive individual. Among (amongst? maybe) those
emotions, I have felt love, that strange concoction of
charity and irritation and expediency and gratitude while
(whilst?) sharing these past few weeks with Hyacinth.
What was it that first attracted me to her? Casting my
mind about, the fish I eventually hook is the fact that she
could offer me something I did not have, something
more valuable than money itself, namely peace of mind.
Never again, I thought, would I have to suffer my own
Camelia's damnable blend of philistinism and
gymnastics. Never again would I initiate a discussion on
Dr Johnson only to be asked whether he could supply cut
price paracetemol at short notice. Never again would I
bring up the venerable Partridge only to be told that he
was best served in a cream and apple sauce. Never again
would I find myself having to leap over a room to catch

my first edition Balzac, thus curtailing its use as an impromptu 'frisbee'.

Though I would hardly describe my own wife as a frying pan, nor yours, my dear Gerald, as a fire, I have indeed gained insight into the efficacy of the aforementioned proverb. Admittedly her Val Doonican impersonation has about it the aroma of brilliance, and the hand trained in Origami extends its skill most cunningly to the undetected acquisition of *bric-à-brac* from stores both large and small. Similarly, her dedication to the rooting out of anagrams from even the most resilient household words (lampshade, Moulinex, staircase) is as singular in its vehemence – at least twenty are tackled each day – as it is in its inventiveness (spam lead, Limousinex, car chase). But, weighed under as I am by this *embarrasse de richesse*, my feelings of guilt have multiplied. Take her back, my dear Gerald, and relieve me of my burden. You deserve her far more than do I.

How very difficult it is to attract the attention of Press and Public to the arrival of a second novel, particularly one as rich and infinitely slight as Kenneth Crabbe's *To Lacedaemon Did My Land Extend*: we have all been racking our brains to mastermind the kind of publicity once vouchsafed to, say, Sylvia Plath. He is a writer of immense promise, and will always be, so the sooner he gets the appropriate attention the better for us all.

Quite an hefty chunk of bon mots I seem to have penned! I hope your postman ('Communications Advisory Officer' nowadays, no doubt!) doesn't crack his back. So delighted that you will soon be with your dear wife once more.

Yours ever,
Harvey

1 October   *Bookends*

My dear Harvey,

That was indeed a wondrous wadge of wit and wisdom which whooped through my wetterbox this very morn!!! I began my perusal of *le Premiere Page* at the outset of breaking fast and it took me right through my Puffa Puffa Rice (Splendid with a dollop of Old Tawny Marmalade plomped a'top); pages two and three found me chomping through what would have been a platter of eggs, bacon, tomatoes, kidneys and Alphabetti Spaghetti had I bothered with the platter (memo to m'self: clean sheets Thursday week!) and pages four, five and six were of such cordiality that my Mellow Birds seemed to have migrated to more frosty climes by the time I set my lips to them (!!!).

I delighted in your delight at my delight at my 'sketch' for Messrs Morecambe and Wise. To keep you giggling through what is to this detached observer obviously a tricky time for you, I submit one further ticklish gem from my appendix, this time written especially for performance by that delightful duo whose performances owe so much to the Music Hall grates – I speak of Little and Large, no less:-

Little:	Are you Large?
Large:	I am indeed, old chum.
Little:	Well if that isn't a funny coincidence. You see, I'm Little.
Large	(*looking down at Little*): Well I can see you're not Large, and that's for sure.
	(*Audience laughter*)

143

Little:	And you're a Little on the Large side.
	(*Audience laughter*)
Large:	And I'm a Large on the Little side.
	(*Audience laughter*)
Little:	We could never switch identities, you know.
Large:	And why not, my good sir?
Little:	Because I'm so Little and you're so Large.
	(*Audience laughter*)

I trust this *petit soupçon* has prompted chuckles galore from aft to fore of your visage. More of my book at a later juncture, but let me first assure you that only over your dead body would I so much as contemplate welshing on our gentleman's agreement that it is on you, my dear Harvey, and none other on whom the lot of publishing my *Pass The Fruitcake, Iris* has fallen and will continue to fall. Though obviously one could make what I believe is known *au trade* as 'a quick killing' by releasing snippets around the world prior to publication, this would do you out of a sizeable pocket of prestige; I might add that I have purely selfish reasons for delaying all 'til publication: now that the entire *œuvre* has grown to something well over a thousand pages, to extract a little bitty here and a little bitty there would cast a most uneven light over the entirety. For instance, an aficionado of Big-Throated Willie The Gumboot Swallower would be understandably disconcerted to be confronted by a clumsily extracted piece which made no mention of that prime act when the heading boldly announced 'Exclusive to *The Daily Blah!* Chapter 39 of Gerald Marsh's New Book – *The East Finchley Odeon and Acts Performing Therein 1905-1910*' No – all at once and once for all, as Camus' vociferous trio were accustomed to yell (!).

I too bubble with pleasure at all things Eastern; like an

hot Indian curry, the Eastern mind exudes sayings that rise into the air, linger awhile and then gently, ever so gently, disappear. I have recently experienced *frissons* of delight whilst thumbing my way through that dependable old tome, the *Kama Sutra*, with all its absurdly contorted methods for achieving what should be the simplest of pastimes. After all, wherein lies the point of bothering with Origami if the very act of folding a piece of paper correctly involves one in back-wrenching gymnastics, of tremendous interest to your (ex!) wife perhaps, but of no use to the more sedentary among us. For why were my *frissons* excited, and whence? My dear Harvey, your perceptive brain, usually a veritable feather-bed of acuity, seems to have gripped hold of what was in my Naval days termed as the wrong end of the lean measure of wood. There are no books that I thumb more thoroughly than those left by Hyacinth, for the sturdiness of their presence attests again and again to the permanence of her absence, and as I have mentioned to you *au passant* in passing – not through any desire to starch the upper lip, I assure you – on my tod I am in an heaven more seventh than that provided by Looming Towers, my private school, and the latter haven was my sanctuary a full seventy years ago. So let your jippy conscience play up no more – you are more than welcome to H. Of course, were you ever to grow awearied of those multifarious activities that occupy so much of H.'s waking hours – I speak not solely of the detecting of metal, the fun and games in the more studiously patrolled supermarkets, the early Burl Ives on the harmonica and the Origami, but also of her more clandestine devotion to the penning of poison pen letters (didn't I tell you?) to national and international 'celebrities', among them many leading figures in the Metropolitan Police – then I feel sure that we could 'come to an arrangement' (ghastly expresh!) whereby I would gain Hyacinth back and you in turn would gain the world rights to my tome (with, need I say, strict, legally enforcible whys and wherefores as to publication date, quantity published and advance payment: I have always found it much more healthy for a friendship to set the legal hounds to work rather than battle it out eye to, as it were, eye). Wasn't it Cecil Parkinson who was in the habit of quoting Winston's dictum, 'Fair swaps'?

I will keep Jackie Kennedy firmly under my belt. A redoubtable man, Janov: I recollect avidly leafing through his earlier book on Edward Kennedy, in which he went a long way towards proving that Mary Jo Kopechne was the first of many victims of the Loch Ness Monster since its emigration to the United States, and his splendid *The Real War*, in which he went a long way towards proving that Adolf Hitler was in fact working for the Allies. My tongue is quite literally rubbing against my chin at the prospect of perusing his latest. How clever of you to snap him up!

It seems that in the last few days the whole world has been huffing and puffing to extract an exclusive interview from me about you and your past and present. I have of course let them know that this is impossible. An interview is, after all, only 'exclusive' if it is given to one person, and I have been jabbering away to the lot of 'em!

Yours ever,
Gerald

2 November 1983   BY HAND

My dear Gerald,

Trusting that your pince-nez are appropriately positioned, you will, I have no doubt, notice that the bearer of this particular missive is quite some way from bearing resemblance to your regular postman, estimable fellow though I am sure that jovial employee of Her Majesty's Postal Service undoubtedly is. No – close scrutiny of the bearer's striking visage will alert you to the fact that it belongs to thine goodly wife, viz Hyacinth of that parish. I attached her to the envelope (are you an *en*velope or an *on*velope man? – I'm a bit of one and a bit of t'other) not purely for the delight of reliving those days when all deliveries were carried by Shanks' pony but also as a means of safely directing her to the delicious domesticity of your doorstep, her rightful home. Lest her presence be for you of only partial pleasure – the image of neat gin springs to mind – I have enclosed an accompanying tonic, to wit, a full and legal contract from my firm offering you a substantial sum for the pleasure and, it must be added, privilege of publishing your splendid *Pass the Fruitcake, Iris* before Autumn of next year.

Entre nous, Hyacinth, who had, for some reason or another, taken quite a shine to me, was reluctant to return to Bookends without some form of – how shall I put it? – consolation prize. She made stalwart use of the unhappy adjective, 'insufficient' at my offerings of, in chronological order, a box of Milk Tray chocolates, a Harrods voucher, a complete set of lightweight suitcases, a life subscription to *The Field*, Premium Bonds to the value of £500, dinner for 20 with the Earl and Countess Spencer, a three week Cunard cruise round the Azores, and, finally, £3500 in hard cash. But she would accept nothing less than the publication of the Cookery Book upon which she claims to have worked for the last twenty years of her life, namely, *The Beauty of Blancmange*. You know how much I care for her, so of course I eventually relented. Though I have yet to set our Cookery Editor onto it, I find it hard to believe that her 'test-outs' of dishes such as Tandoori Blancmange or Blancmange Fritters or Chocolate Blancmange will amount to anything remotely palatable, particularly as she insists that for the latter recipe the silver paper and outer wrapping must be thrown in as well. I would be undying in my gratitude were you to dissuade her from her more *outré* concoctions, my dear Gerald.

Alas and alack, I am forced to curtail this all-too-brief 'note' as I am overdue for the tribute being paid me by the mass media of the world. Little Melvyn Bragg will be there with his 'Arts Aplenty!' crew, but he will have to share the questioning and the compliments with at least twenty others now. I am told the clamour will be such that I will exit under police escort. At long last, a decent English publisher will be getting his just deserts! (Wasn't it Alan Coren who (intentionally) mistook them for just *desserts*, and went off into a marvellously Goonish reverie about how he wanted a main course? Delightful!)

Yours ever,
Harvey

P.S. Sadly Kenneth Crabbe died from falling typewriter

wounds early yesterday. Already, *The Sunday Times* is planning a major feature around his life and times, and Kaleidoscope is devoting an entire programme to him tomorrow, on the eve of the publication of his second novel. A major talent, and sorely missed.

P.P.S. The Den is an anagram for The Edn.

Index

INDEX